ALL IN

ALL | IN

WHAT IT TAKES TO BE THE BEST

GENE CHIZIK

with DAVID THOMAS

TYNDALE HOUSE PUBLISHERS, INC.

CAROL STREAM, ILLINOIS

Visit Tyndale online at www.tyndale.com.

TYNDALE and Tyndale's quill logo are registered trademarks of Tyndale House Publishers, Inc.

All In: What It Takes to Be the Best

Designed by Daniel Farrell

Edited by Stephanie Voiland

Published in association with the literary agency of Working Title Agency LLC, Spring Hill, TN.

Library of Congress Cataloging-in-Publication Data

Chizik, Gene.
    All in : what it takes to be the best / Gene Chizik with David Thomas.
      p. cm.
    ISBN 978-1-4143-6435-3 (hc)
    1. Success—Religious aspects—Christianity. 2. Chizik, Gene. 3. Football fans—Religious life.
I. Thomas, David, date. II. Title.
    BV4598.3.C5 2011
    248.8'8092—dc23
    [B]   2011020852

Printed in the United States of America

17   16   15   14   13   12   11
7   6   5   4   3   2

DEDICATION

This book is dedicated to the four most important people in my life: my beautiful wife, Jonna; my daughters, Landry and Kennedy; and my son, Cally. I know how much all of you have sacrificed so Daddy can be a coach. Not many people understand those sacrifices, but I surely do. I know you guys always have my back—even when "Coach" is seemingly not doing a very good job.

Jonna, you are the rock of our family. You have stood by me through the long hours, the hectic schedules, and the less-than-desirable Valentine's gifts. You are my inspiration and have shown me what it looks like to truly have a servant's heart.

Landry, it has been a blessing for me to see your spirit and your ability to captivate those around you. Your heart is the thing that separates you from most—the way you try to protect me is incredible and much appreciated. You are your mom reincarnated.

Kennedy, I admire your insight and commitment to excellence. You amaze me with your organization and attention to details. Your dry sense of humor and quick wit keep me smiling all the time. You remind me of your daddy when I was little.

And my boy, Cally. You have fulfilled every aspect of what your name represents—a legacy to be proud of. You are a wonderful kid: talented, smart, and so much fun. I believe the YouTube video of you dancing in the locker room probably received more hits than my press conference after the National Championship Game. Your manners and polite gestures have an impact on everyone around you, and I know you will be a tremendous leader. You will always be my boy!

You all have shown me what it truly means to be all in. I love you.

CONTENTS

FOREWORD

ONE OF MY EARLIEST MEMORIES of Gene and Jonna Chizik is from the first time Gene brought his son, Cally, then five years old, to our Longhorn football offices. Chip Robertson, our equipment manager, brought some Texas gear to give to the kids, and among the items was a small football. Politely, Cally asked, "Can I throw this football with my dad?"

Gene's moment with his son demonstrated one of the significant pieces of what my wife, Sally, and I have come to believe is the most important foundation in a person's life—that it should be built on faith, family, and friends. And of course, in our business, you can add one more *f*—football.

In that moment, what I saw in Gene was his love for and devotion to his family. It obviously came from his roots. From a dad who was a proud Marine, Gene had learned the value of discipline, and he also got a good dose of loyalty at the same time.

In the 2005 season, with Gene as our defensive coordinator, we won the Rose Bowl and the BCS National Championship in a 41–38 victory over Southern Cal. While our quarterback, Vince Young, earned credit and respect that night in Pasadena, the fact was that it took a defensive stop on a fourth down with just a couple of minutes left in the game for us to even have a chance.

On that fourth down play, Gene and our defense found their inspiration from a source that his dad would have been proud of—it is part of the creed of every Marine who ever fought, and it is part of the fiber that is handed down to their children. In that moment our defense wasn't fighting for Texas or for its fans or even for the national championship that we wanted so badly. Every player and every coach was fighting for each other.

Gene's faith has always been an inspiration. His love and devotion to his family are evident in everything he does. As he forms friendships, he employs the principles we share at Texas. We have built our program on communication, trust, and respect, as well as a common purpose. That combination works for a football team, and it also works in life.

I knew from the moment Gene and Jonna came into our lives at Texas that his destiny was to become a great head coach. To make that happen, he wasn't afraid to accept challenges, and he never paid attention to what others said and thought. He would seek advice, of course, but ultimately he knew where he was going, and he knew what he would do to get there.

In the end, he returned to his roots when he went back to Auburn. He knew Auburn's tradition, and he knew he wanted to be a part of it. It was there that he secured the final piece of our team goal—a common purpose. And it was there, with everybody pulling together, that he achieved his dream.

MACK BROWN
Head football coach, the University of Texas at Austin

PROLOGUE

IT WAS THE INTERVIEW I had been waiting for my entire life. My dream job. The head football coaching position at Auburn University. Unfortunately the dream was quickly turning into a waking nightmare.

As my wife, Jonna, eased the car up to the hotel entrance, I struggled through the passenger door and gingerly pulled myself to a standing position. The pain was excruciating. I strained to reach behind my back and tuck my white dress shirt into my light-gray suit pants again, still feeling the aftereffects of the back surgery I had undergone only two days earlier. *Man,* I thought to myself, *this is not how I had planned to walk into this thing.*

On the bright side, at least I didn't have to worry about how my back would handle the usual load of notebooks, calendars, recruiting plans, training schedules, laptop, and other presentation pieces I had carried into previous interviews for head coaching positions. This interview had come about so quickly I'd barely had time to begin pulling my notes together the previous night. And frankly, what I *had* been able to get down on paper wasn't looking all that great to me.

In fact, after closer inspection, I decided to just scrap my notes entirely. All one page of them. *Whatever,* I thought, wadding up the page and tossing it into the backseat. *They know who I am. I'm just going to have to go with what I know.* And if there was one thing I knew, it was football—*Auburn* football.

Once inside the hotel, I shuffled as quickly as I could through the lobby and made my way toward the small conference room that Auburn had reserved for its interviews, hoping my slow pace wouldn't give anyone enough time to recognize me. That's all it would take for ESPN to start scrolling a "Chizik Interviews for Auburn Job" headline across the bottom of television screens all over the country—especially back home in Iowa. A news leak was about the only missing element that would have turned this scenario into a complete nightmare for me.

So with a throbbing back, no notes, and a mind that a meteorologist would have reported as "mostly cloudy" at best, I staggered toward that small meeting room, knowing that the Auburn search committee was already seated around the table and there was an empty chair waiting for me. It was my turn to try to impress upon the committee members that I was the right man for their job.

Thankfully Jonna hadn't mentioned to me that, on top of everything else, my skin still had kind of a postsurgical greenish tint to it. I suppose she figured I had enough on my mind already. Between a hectic recruiting schedule, my surgery, and now the painkiller-aided recovery, there simply hadn't been enough time to assemble a formal presentation detailing how I would lead the Auburn Tigers to a national championship. Still, with more than two decades of coaching experience behind me, including three recent postseason bowl game appearances as Auburn's defensive coordinator and a national championship with the University of Texas as assistant coach and co–defensive coordinator, I was more than confident in my ability to do this job and do it right. I might not have had any fancy handouts or PowerPoint presentations with me that afternoon, but in many ways, I had been preparing for this interview for the past twenty years. *Bring it on,* I thought, opening the door to the conference room. *I'm ready.*

As soon as I entered the room, I breathed a slight sigh of relief. As it turned out, all the committee members around the table had been at Auburn when I was the defensive coordinator there four years earlier, so I knew they'd be able to look beyond my less-than-stellar physical appearance that day . . . including my Grinch-like skin.

These guys knew me. They knew I understood everything there was to know about Auburn—the school, its football program, and its fans. They knew I steadfastly believed in doing things not just the right way but the *Auburn* way. They knew I could coach. And they knew I could win.

But there was one factor they could not overlook: my 5–19 record in my two seasons as head coach at Iowa State. That was going to be a tough hurdle to clear—especially in my current state.

As expected, it took only a few minutes for my record to come up.

"If we hire you as the head coach at Auburn, Gene," one of the interviewers asked, leaning forward in his chair and staring at me intently, "how in the world are we going to explain it to the public?"

The other committee members' eyes fastened to me. The looks on their faces told me this could be a make-or-break answer.

I took a deep breath.

Now that, I thought to myself, *is a great question.*

1

THE JOURNEY BEGINS

AS SOON AS the interview was over, I stepped outside to call Jonna.

"Baby, I think I got it."

It was 2006. Iowa State University was looking for a head coach, and I was looking for my first head coaching job.

The biggest question facing me was, if Iowa State *did* offer me the job, should I take it?

The biggest question that friends, colleagues, and members of the media would be asking me in the weeks ahead was, "Gene, *why* did you take that job?"

Back when I first interviewed with Iowa State, I was considered one of the hottest head coaching prospects in college football. I was one game away from finishing my second season as assistant head coach, co–defensive coordinator, and linebackers coach at the University of Texas, where we had just won a national championship the year before and were now poised to finish the 2006 regular season with a 9–3 record and to earn the program's ninth consecutive postseason bowl appearance.

Prior to that, I had spent three years as defensive coordinator at Auburn, where in my final season we compiled a perfect 13–0 record, won the Southeastern Conference Championship, and went on to defeat Virginia Tech in the Sugar Bowl. That same year I received the Broyles Award, presented annually to the nation's top assistant coach.

General consensus was that I was going to land my first head coaching job, and soon. General consensus also held that Iowa State was not the best place for that to happen.

In a way, the general consensus was right. As much as I wanted to become a head coach, I initially had some pretty strong reservations about the possibility of taking over the reins at Iowa State.

Aside from a brief streak of successful seasons under their most recent coach, Dan McCarney, Iowa State was not known for having a winning tradition in football. As the school's longest-tenured coach at twelve seasons, Dan was also Iowa State's all-time winningest coach. Heading into 2006, Coach McCarney had led his teams to at least seven wins and a bowl game in five of the previous six seasons. But before that the Cyclones had made only four bowl appearances, and the school had been playing football for more than one hundred years. When a team doesn't have a string of winning records behind it, the already-difficult job of recruiting top talent becomes that much harder.

Plus, the Big 12 Conference is a very tough conference, and it might have been at its strongest during that time period. In addition to Texas, Iowa State had to contend with traditional powerhouses such as Oklahoma and Nebraska, not to mention a number of programs that were on the rise, like Kansas, Missouri, and Texas Tech, to name a few. Whoever stepped into the Iowa State coaching job was going to have a tough road ahead of him if he wanted to build up the program to become consistently competitive in the Big 12.

From a personal standpoint, Jonna and I wrestled with the fact that we had never lived that far north—in fact, we'd never lived farther north than Tennessee. For that matter, neither of us had ever even *been* to Iowa. We had to look up Ames on a map, and when we learned that Canada was only a nine-hour drive from there, we realized how far from our home state of Florida we would be. Since our entire immediate and extended families lived down South, we knew we'd be completely on our own if we decided to make the move. Not to mention the fact that if I took the job, it would be the third time in five years that I would have to uproot my family. The kids would have to say good-bye to all their friends . . . again, change schools . . . again, and learn a whole new routine . . . again. And because I would be working ridiculously long hours and constantly on the road recruiting, Jonna would be left to pack, unpack, and set up a new house in a strange city, with no friends, family, or support network to lean on. There were a lot of challenges, both personal and professional, to take into consideration.

Shortly after Coach McCarney announced in early November that he would be resigning at the end of the 2006 season (in which the Cyclones ended up finishing 4–8), I received a call from Dan Parker of the search firm Baker Parker and Associates, asking if I would be interested in a head coaching vacancy at a Bowl Championship Series–level school.

"Of course I would," I told him.

I had been steadily working my way up through the coaching ranks for years, and at age forty-four I felt like I had attained all the goals I had set for myself as an assistant coach. I firmly believed I was ready to become a head coach. Granted, I had envisioned that the opening would be at a school with an established winning program (or at least one that was on the verge of winning regularly), but I figured at the very least, interviewing with Iowa State would be a good learning experience for me. So with Texas coach Mack Brown's blessing, I accepted the invitation to interview with Iowa State's athletic director and associate athletic director.

The interview was set for the following week. It was technically an off week for the Longhorns, but you'd never have guessed it. We were using every minute to prepare for our final game of the regular season against our archrival, Texas A&M.

Some coaches like to have their names floated out in the media as head coaching candidates, hoping the publicity will boost their careers. But I prefer not to have that kind of attention around me. I like to be able to focus on the job at hand. I didn't want the distraction of having to answer questions from the media and deal with speculation about my job prospects during such a critical point in our season. Our team was looking to win the Big 12's South Division title and earn a spot in the conference championship game, and the last thing I or the team needed was a lot of extraneous media attention disturbing our focus. Interview or not, winning that final game against the Aggies was my number one priority. I was bound and determined to keep it that way.

GOING TO IOWA . . . VIA DALLAS

We arranged to hold the interview in Dallas to help keep things confidential. In addition to the possibility of a job candidate being sighted near a university other than his own, there is also the risk that a media member or a school alum will use public information to track airplane destinations. If Iowa State had flown me from Austin, Texas, to Ames for the interview, someone could have picked up on the flight itinerary and connected the dots to discover that I was a candidate for the job. Dallas makes a good place for such meetings because of its size and central location; plus, with Southern Methodist University, Texas Christian University, and the Dallas Cowboys all located in the Dallas/ Fort Worth area and other large college football programs not far from the Metroplex, there are plenty of rabbit trails around to throw off the hounds. I know all that secrecy seems crazy, but when it comes to monitoring head coaching job searches, the interest really is that intense.

To make sure the interview didn't interfere with our practice schedule, I arranged to drive to Dallas the night before the interview and leave as soon as it ended. I'd be back at work in Austin shortly after lunch.

I was prepared down to the last detail. I went in armed with my short-term plan, my long-term plan, my calendar for how my schedule would look as soon as I took the job (if they offered and I accepted), my mission statement, and all those things you think might impress during a job interview. For two hours the athletic director and his assistant quizzed me about everything you could think of regarding the running of a college football program.

They wanted to know my philosophy for recruiting players to their school. I told them my first emphasis would be on players from the state of Iowa. My research had told me that the rival University of Iowa was signing more high school players from the state than Iowa State was, and I made clear my intention to match them for in-state recruits. Outside of Iowa, I would use my connections in talent-rich Florida and Texas to bring speed players into the program.

The athletic officials also wanted to know what kind of coaching staff I would put together. I said I didn't want them to focus too much on the specific places I'd be hiring from. I wasn't concerned with trying to wow them by saying I'd bring on staff from, say, the Denver Broncos or the New York Giants. In fact, I said I'd probably be hiring some coaches whose names they hadn't heard. I was going to hire a great staff who I knew could coach football well, would work hard, and would make it a priority to recruit quality athletes and upstanding young men. My basic message to the athletic director and his assistant was, "Trust me. I'm going to hire the best guys for the job whether you've heard of them or not."

They also asked my immediate plan if I became their head coach. I laid out my first month's plan from the day I would step onto campus, including meeting with the team's players to introduce myself and communicate my expectations to them, and meeting with the current coaching staff and deciding who would stay on with me. I also presented my three-month plan and my one-year plan, casting a vision for where I saw the future of the program at those points into my tenure.

I had prepared every detail for every question I anticipated they might ask. I hadn't been a head coach before, but I wanted to show them I had thought through exactly how my first program would look. I knew I was ready to become a head coach.

After answering the interviewers' questions, I asked them questions for an hour. As that hour progressed, and as my questions about the school and the program were answered to my satisfaction, the possibility of coaching at Iowa State began to make more and more sense. Perhaps the largest potential stumbling block was how much the school was willing to put in the recruiting budget to bring in the athletes I believed the team would need, as well as the amount of money they were prepared to spend to hire the assistant coaches we would need. But after talking through some details that day, I felt satisfied that the commitment level I sought was there.

Another important issue to me that I discussed at the interview was my desire to create a team chaplain position. That idea was met with full approval, and as the interview went on, I was hearing everything I needed to hear—and honestly hadn't expected to hear—to convince me that not only was Iowa State a place I could be head coach, but it was also a place that wanted to build a winning football program and was serious about putting in the effort to get there.

I felt confident throughout the interview, and at the conclusion I was told I could expect to be contacted in four or five days. As soon as I left the building, I called Jonna.

"Baby, I think I got it," I said.

"Really?" she asked. "How do you know?"

"I just have a good feeling about it," I answered.

The next day Dan Parker called and told me that Iowa State wanted me to meet with the school's president for a second interview. In Dallas, of course. It was understood that the second interview would not take place until after our game with Texas A&M and that there would be no more conversations about the job until the interview. I didn't want anything to distract me from that final game.

Unfortunately, in spite of all our preparation, we lost our

final game of the regular season 12–7 to Texas A&M on the day after Thanksgiving. It's always a bitter defeat when Texas loses to the Aggies, and missing out on a chance to play for the conference title made that loss even more painful. Even so, our 9–3 record gave us the opporunity to play in the Alamo Bowl in San Antonio, Texas.

By the time the bowl game rolls around, I wondered, *where will I be?* I wouldn't have guessed it then, but as it turned out, I'd be living in a hotel in Ames. And I'd be head coach of the Iowa State Cyclones.

Jonna went with me for the second interview. It was a Saturday, the day after the A&M game, when we met with Jamie Pollard, Iowa State's athletic director, and Gregory Geoffroy, the school's president. It wasn't until later, when Jamie and I were reflecting on the interviews, that I learned they had worked out a signal for the president to indicate whether he liked me and approved of hiring me. I can't remember for sure, but it was something like President Geoffroy's scratching the lapel on his suit jacket or rubbing the Iowa State pin he was wearing. Jamie laughed when he told me that, shortly into the interview, the president gave his signal of approval.

After we chatted briefly, they offered me the job and a contract for six years with more than $1 million in annual salary. I was caught slightly off guard by being offered the job on the spot. And although Jonna and I have always kept our priorities in line when it comes to money, hearing *million* attached to *dollars* certainly caught our attention.

The athletic director and the president wanted to give us time to make our decision, so the interview ended there. Of course, Jonna and I had much to discuss. Based on the answers to my questions during the first interview, and having those answers affirmed in the meeting with the school president, we both believed that a winning program could be built at Iowa State. As an assistant and a coordinator, I had been part of too many successful traditions to think otherwise. And during the interviews, it became clear that the school officials were 100 percent committed to creating a strong, championship-caliber program. Going to Iowa State made sense to us—from a football standpoint, at least.

It would still mean a big move—and uprooting Jonna and the kids—but we'd done it before. And while it wouldn't be easy, we knew that if we needed to, we could do it again.

But these two pieces were only part of the equation.

As deeply spiritual people, Jonna and I agreed that we would not make the move unless we felt confident that it was what God wanted us to do. Since fielding the first phone call from Dan Parker, we had prayed on a regular basis about the Iowa State opening. The time between the two interviews allowed us plenty of time to pray and discuss the situation together. At each step of the process, we continued to ask God to give us confirmation—that "gut feeling"—whether we should accept the job if it was offered. Iowa State hadn't made a lot of sense to us at first, but ever since the first interview, the job was becoming increasingly attractive to us.

I have always loved being a coach, but to me, coaching is about so much more than X's and O's. Don't get me wrong. I am extremely competitive, and I love to win. (Just ask my three children about our family game nights.) But I also see my job as a ministry and an opportunity to have a deep and lasting impact on kids' lives—whether those kids are in Austin, Auburn, or as it turned out, Ames.

After praying it over and talking to Coach Brown, Jonna and I were confident that God was calling us to Iowa State. Coach Brown agreed that it would be best to leave the team before the Alamo Bowl so I could get started at my new job.

I know there were plenty of people—other coaches and media, particularly—who were scratching their heads over our decision. To them, Iowa State didn't appear to be the logical next stop on my career track. They would have advised me that the annual merry-go-round of coaching vacancies would soon kick into high gear as teams finished their regular seasons, and among those would be programs with histories of winning that Iowa State did not offer. And in case one of those jobs didn't come up, I could have stayed at Texas, where each year the team has an opportunity to win eleven, twelve, thirteen games and be in contention for a national championship. Either way, sooner or not much later, I would have been able to practically handpick the school for my first head coaching job. But we were completely convinced that this job was an opportunity God was providing for us, and we believed wholeheartedly there was a reason he wanted us at Iowa State.

It might not have made a lot of sense to people on the outside, but from the inside looking out, it made all the sense in the world.

MY SPIRITUAL JOURNEY

As significant as my coaching journey is in my life, my relationship with Jesus Christ is even more important. In fact, in many ways, my spiritual journey has defined who I am as a coach.

I grew up Catholic, and Jonna grew up Methodist. We got married in 1996, and you'll enjoy the story I tell in a later chapter about how we met. After the wedding, we discussed whether I should attend a Methodist church or Jonna should become Catholic. We attended various churches together, but we never seemed to settle on one that we felt would help forge our spiritual identity as a couple. Then, about a decade ago, while I was coaching at the University of Central Florida in Orlando, we found a church we both liked. The services were different from the churches either of us had attended before. Partly because of that, it provided the groundwork for the spiritual identity we had been seeking as a couple. This wasn't Jonna coming to my church or me going to hers. It became *our* church, and it was there that my faith really began to grow.

I had always believed in God, and on a certain level, I always knew that he had a plan for my life. But now, for the first time, I was beginning to grasp that there was a deeper purpose to my life than just being a football coach. As I listened to other people talk about their relationships with Christ, I felt a hunger to pursue a richer spiritual journey myself.

Among other things, I began to understand that we have been placed on earth not to be served but rather to serve others. I also came to understand that God put each of us here for a specific reason—in my case, to help shape the lives of young men who play football.

It wasn't long before we moved to Alabama, where I had accepted a job as defensive coordinator/defensive backs coach at Auburn University. There were two significant spiritual developments that occurred during my first coaching tenure there.

First, we began attending Victory World Prayer Center in Auburn. We remained in the background at first, sitting near the back during services and not taking part in many of the church functions. But as our children became more involved in kids' activities at the church, Jonna and I started developing a relationship with the pastor, Mike Wright, and his wife, Sue. They quickly became great friends, but more than that, they ended up being mentors to Jonna and me. The timing could not have been better.

Our second year at Auburn, 2003, was a difficult one professionally, and it ended up bleeding into our personal lives as well. We entered that season with high expectations, having been ranked number one in the country by some voters in the preseason polls. But then we lost our first game 23–0 to the University of Southern California. At home, no less. Then we lost the following week at Georgia Tech. The 0–2 start dropped us out of the top twenty-five rankings and effectively ended our hopes of winning a national championship. We managed to bounce back and win our next five games, putting us back in the national rankings, but we followed that with another poor stretch in which we lost three of our next four games.

Not surprisingly, with our team failing to live up to preseason expectations, speculation erupted that our head coach, Tommy Tuberville, might soon be replaced. When a head coach loses his job, typically his assistants do too. With Tommy's job on the line, all our jobs were in jeopardy. And believe me, that led to a few sleepless nights at the Chizik household. What if they let Tommy go? Who would they bring in to take his place? Would we have to leave? Where would we go?

Tommy ended up retaining his job at Auburn, but dealing with all the uncertainty that season took its toll on the entire coaching staff, including me. And Jonna.

Even under the best of circumstances, being a college-level

coach comes with its share of pressures. Our children were young at the time—our twin daughters, Landry and Kennedy, were in kindergarten, and our son, Cally, was just a toddler. I wasn't home much because of my job, which meant Jonna was shouldering the bulk of the child-rearing stress on her own.

I love my job. But I also love my family, and unfortunately one of the downsides of coaching at this level is the amount of family time you have to give up. Between recruiting, off-season practices, the regular season, and—if things go well—bowl games, we are basically on the go year-round. Most days I'm at the office early and I don't get home until late—I usually put in a sixteen- or seventeen-hour day. From August 1 until the first Wednesday of February (National Signing Day), we pretty much run nonstop—no days off, no holidays, no breaks. Add a bowl game into the mix, and there goes Christmas and possibly New Year's.

Over the years, I have had both the great fortune and the great misfortune of having to reassure my kids that "Yes, Santa will be able to find us here at the hotel tonight!" There's no question—it's a fantastic job, and I absolutely love it, but it's also a grind. As a result, Jonna is pretty much a single parent six to seven months a year.

At any rate, with both of us under so much pressure at the same time, we knew we needed people we could lean on—people with whom we could close the door and say, "Hey, this is where we're at, and we need some help." The Wrights filled that role for us, and we weren't too bashful or too proud to go to them with our needs. We really leaned on them during those early years, soaking up their advice and insights. One of the themes they kept repeating to us was how big our God is, and during that stressful time, we trusted in that big God and felt his peace comforting us amid all the rumors, speculation, and turmoil we were facing.

A couple of years after we plugged into their church, the Wrights announced that they were leaving Auburn to enter foreign missions work. It was a tremendous shock and a disappointment to say good-bye to these people who had become such an integral part of our lives and had helped guide us through a rich time of spiritual growth. But as is often the case in the coaching business, it wasn't long before we, too, were moving on—this time to Texas, where I'd signed on with the Texas Longhorns.

A LASTING INFLUENCE

That period of spiritual growth under the Wrights' mentorship proved to be a major turning point in my life because for the first time I felt like I was gaining a true relationship with God. Again, it wasn't that I didn't know God was there before—I had prayed regularly since I was a little kid. But now I realized that I was able to talk with God and sense his guiding presence inside me. It's a difficult thing to explain, especially to people who have never had that type of connection with God, but I can assure you it is real and it is life changing. It didn't take long before the people who were around me the most started to see that there was something different about me.

I soon realized, however, that it wasn't enough for me to keep this relationship between just me and God. One day in 2002, not long after we moved to Auburn, Mike said to me, "Gene, look at the opportunity you have to change kids' lives." I had always treated my players fairly, and I'd always been up front and honest with them. But with Mike's one sentence, God's purpose for me as a football coach became clear.

I believe God has blessed me with the ability to be a good coach. He has given me football instincts and knowledge that could only come from him. I also have been given the gift of being able to communicate with players. I know my players; I can read their body language. And that helps me sense what they are thinking and feeling—when they're confident and, more important, when they're really struggling.

But why have I been given these abilities? The more time I spent listening to that guiding presence inside me, the more clearly I was able to see the purpose behind those gifts. Mike's words drove home the opportunity I'd been given: to influence eighteen- to twenty-two-year-olds who are being exposed to everything from A to Z in college.

Because of my coaching abilities and the doors that have opened as a result, I have the chance to make a significant impact on those young men. Because of that, I can have an influence on their futures that extends far beyond football.

Since 2002, my mission has been to develop godly young men who will become good men, good husbands, and good fathers in a society that is woefully lacking in those roles. I have a platform from which I can teach them the value of real winning—being a positive addition to society, serving others, making a difference in the world, and being a leader both on and off the field.

As God began to shape my vision for serving him as a coach, he brought another key person into my life—a man by the name of Chette Williams.

Chette was the team chaplain when I came to Auburn in 2002. He played football at Auburn in the 1980s and graduated with a degree in adult education, then went on to earn a master's of divinity from New Orleans Baptist Theological Seminary. In my first tenure at Auburn, I was inspired as I watched Chette work with young men in the football program, many of whom had come from dysfunctional backgrounds. A number of players told me that until they came to Auburn, they'd never had someone like Chette to turn to for spiritual guidance. He offered them wise, godly counsel, just as the Wrights had done for Jonna and me.

As I watched Chette's role in transforming the guys during those three years at Auburn, I thought, *Now that is what it's all about right there.* Like any assistant coach with plans to one day become a head coach, I was compiling mental notes of how I would run my own program when the time came. Based on my observations of Chette and the impact I saw him having on our players, I decided that when I became a head coach, the first thing I'd do would be to make sure my program had a team chaplain. If there wasn't one, I would get one.

So when I took over at Iowa State, I got down to my first order of business. And let me tell you, I was totally unprepared for the controversy that would create.

There's a valuable lesson to be learned here. Just because you are following the path you believe God has laid out for you does not mean the journey will be easy. Nor does it guarantee you will win a national championship, or whatever the equivalent is in your profession. But committing to a journey with God *does* lead to victory—even though that victory may not be what other people would consider a win.

I know, because that has been my journey.

2

HELLO, 'CLONES!

THE FIRST TIME I set foot on the Iowa State campus was as head coach of the Cyclones.

Because both of my interviews had taken place in Dallas, I'd never had the opportunity to visit the campus or see the athletic facilities. That's a pretty bizarre circumstance for a new head coach. When I had interviewed for assistant coaching positions, I had always visited each prospective school before taking the job. Accepting the Iowa State job campus unseen was uncharted territory for me, but because both the school and I wanted to keep my interviews a secret, it was the only way.

I was uncomfortable with the thought of news leaking about my interview. I didn't want people assuming that I was out chasing jobs while getting paid by another university. I don't chase jobs; I've been fortunate throughout my career to have schools contact me to see if I'd be interested in working for them. I didn't want people at Texas who had treated me well to wrongly believe that I didn't want to be at their school or that my focus was on some other job rather than on my current one. That's just not the way I operate. So not visiting Ames before becoming head coach was odd, yes, and it wasn't the way I would have preferred things to happen. But that was the route we needed to take.

On top of not seeing the campus or athletic facilities, I'd never even been to Iowa State for a game—either as a coach or as a player. School officials were doing all they could to keep the media off our trail until the surprise announcement, which they were planning to make the day after I officially accepted the offer. And they were doing a pretty good job, too. The night before we were scheduled to leave Austin for Iowa, Jonna and I enjoyed quite a laugh when we were watching TV and a sports network reported that Iowa State's next coach would be Brian Kelly, who at the time was the head coach at Central Michigan University. Having our pending news still under wraps felt like a victory of sorts. I can't guess what Coach Kelly must have been thinking at that moment, hearing the report that he was accepting a job he had not been offered!

To keep my identity concealed until I arrived for the big announcement, the school contracted a private plane—former Dallas Cowboys great Troy Aikman's plane, no less—to fly Jonna and me from Austin into Ames. Somehow, though, by the time we were en route, the news had leaked that I was being flown in to be named the Cyclones coach. As we landed, we could see what looked like about a dozen reporters and television camera crews waiting for us, lined up behind a fence set off from the runway. So much for the surprise.

A car picked us up on the tarmac, and we were whisked away from the waiting media directly to athletic director Jamie Pollard's house, where we spent a few hours meeting school officials and relaxing before that night's introduction.

From the moment our feet touched the ground in Ames, Iowa State rolled out the red carpet for us. The public welcoming at the school's indoor sports arena was a huge celebration, complete with giant cardinal-colored inflatable helmets with the Cyclones logo on the sides. Smoke machines were cranked up and blasting giant plumes of smoke as I was introduced. I couldn't make out the public address announcer's words, so I missed how it sounded to be introduced for the first time as a head coach. But as I walked through one of the helmets, I was shocked to see that even with the short notice, a few thousand people had come to show their support. While I continued onto the Hilton Coliseum floor, the fans were cheering loudly, the school's marching band was playing, and the cheerleaders were encouraging the fans to cheer even louder, if that were possible.

"I'm still expecting a rock star or somebody to come out behind me," I said when I stepped to the microphone. "This is truly a blessing."

It truly was. Jonna and I were blown away by the love and appreciation we felt. The fans that night were further proof of Iowa State's commitment to building a strong football program. After being recruited to come to Ames, I couldn't think of a more satisfying way to kick off my first night as head coach.

THE REBUILDING BEGINS

As soon as the welcome ceremony came to a close, I went right to work. A new coach faces two immediate tasks once he takes over: hiring a coaching staff and recruiting players. Knowing that practically all my time would be consumed with those responsibilities, I made a hotel in Ames my temporary home while Jonna and the kids wrapped things up back in Texas. Even though the move was inevitable, Jonna and I wanted to give the kids as much time as we could to adjust. It's hard enough having to say goodbye to your friends when you're nine and six years old. As much as we would have preferred to stay together as a family, we didn't want to compound their agony by yanking them out of school without any notice. So the kids stayed in their schools in the Austin area until spring break, when we were reunited in Iowa.

In building my coaching staff, I tapped heavily into my almost two decades of networking in college football. From the Iowa State coaching staff, I kept Todd Fitch as quarterbacks coach, although he left a few months later to become an offensive coordinator at East Carolina University. I also retained Erik Link, who had been a graduate assistant coach, as an assistant director of football operations, and Mike Motl stayed on as video coordinator. Aside from those exceptions, our staff was brand new to Iowa State.

My first outside hire was Robert McFarland as offensive coordinator. Robert resigned as head coach at Stephen F. Austin in Texas to join me in Ames. I had worked on staff with Robert during my six years at SFA in the 1990s, and we later spent a couple of years together at Central Florida. Robert was a friend as well as a colleague—he had been in my wedding and was a pallbearer at my father's funeral.

My next hire was Wayne Bolt as defensive coordinator. We had worked together in 1988 and 1989 at Clemson, where he was an assistant coach and I was a graduate assistant/linebackers coach making the jump from high school assistant coach into the college ranks. Although that was our only time on a staff together, Wayne and I had remained in touch through the years and often met during off-seasons for three or four days at a time to study football together.

In Robert and Wayne, I was able to hire coaches I knew well, who knew me well—guys I could fully trust. I don't hire coaches because they're friends, but with these men I had the luxury of being able to hire great coaches I'd had the privilege of being close friends with for roughly twenty years.

The trust factor within the coaching staff was huge because my plan was to tear down Iowa State's program and start rebuilding. I had to have coaches I knew were completely on board with what I wanted to do—and could help me carry out that plan.

When I met with the players for the first time, I laid down expectations and a set of standards that were very high. And I mean *very* high. Our players were going to be fine representatives of our school on and off the field. I wanted to find out who really wanted to play football at Iowa State, and I purposely made it sound as though it would be difficult for them to meet my expectations. As a new coach laying down the law like that, you expect to have players who don't want to hear and aren't willing to live up to what you're preaching. To be brutally honest, we didn't want those guys in our program. Those types of players would only hold us back from achieving what we were setting out to accomplish in Ames.

Complicating matters for us was a detail called the Academic Progress Rate (APR). Each year teams receive an APR score based on the eligibility, retention, and graduation of their student-athletes. Teams must meet the NCAA's required minimum score or face the loss of scholarships. Although it's called a progress rate, in effect it's a dropout rate. When players leave a program for whatever reason, the team's APR suffers. Iowa State's APR was a little closer to the minimum score than we would have liked when I arrived. So while I was intentional about pointing out the exit door for players who weren't going to buy into what we were selling, I also had to walk the fine line of not running off too many players and putting us in danger of falling below the minimum score. We did have players leave the program that season, but we stayed above the APR minimum and started our off-season knowing that the players who stuck with the program really wanted to be there.

I met with each player individually in my first days on the job. The problem I recognized immediately was that the players didn't believe they could win a championship. Of course, Iowa State had not won a football championship in almost a century, but we as a coaching staff were determined to change that, and we needed the players to believe it could happen. I had just come from Texas, where we had won a national title two seasons earlier, and the sense throughout the Longhorns program was that every season should be a championship season. If Iowa State was going to win a championship in our conference, we would have to compete with Texas and other schools with that kind of mentality. But winning a title seemed like a foreign concept to our players. That was a place they had never been, and they didn't believe it was within their reach. I saw that as a problem we needed to work on changing immediately.

Because of attrition and graduation, we had a number of slots to fill. To begin with, we had to replace four of our five offensive linemen. It's always a challenge having to replace that many members of an offense's anchor. We did, however, have players we thought we could build around. Alvin "Ace" Bowen was a senior linebacker from New Jersey who had led the nation in tackles the previous season. Ace had the tough mentality I was looking for. He didn't feel like anybody on the field was better than he was. We had Todd Blythe, an Iowan and a senior wide receiver. Big 12 coaches had selected Todd for first-team all-conference as a junior. He was a leader, and the other players on the team followed him. Kurtis Taylor was a junior defensive lineman and another of our players from an Iowa high school. Kurtis was a tough kid who, like Ace Bowen, had the no-quit mentality we wanted to be characteristic of our program. Those were three of the key players who bought into our program's goals from the start, and for a new coach, it is huge to have players you didn't recruit not only accept your coming into the program but also rally the returning players around your philosophy.

Assembling our first recruiting class proved to be a challenge, especially since I didn't have a single connection in the Midwest. Iowa high schools were going to be my primary focus, and I didn't know one high school coach in the state. I spent my first couple of weeks calling ten to fifteen Iowa high school coaches per day simply to introduce myself. High school football in Iowa is a little different from Texas, where I had just recruited heavily for the Longhorns, and Florida, where I had grown up and had a number of built-in connections. In Iowa, it wasn't uncommon to come across a high school football head coach who was a farmer during the day before arriving at school at three o'clock for football practice. That made it difficult to reach some coaches by phone. But I wasn't going to give up easily. I set out to call the most successful coaches first and start the process of building relationships with our in-state coaches.

In the meantime, I was assembling my coaching staff. As assistants came on board, they began helping me recruit right away. It was early December when I hired Robert McFarland as my first assistant coach. National Signing Day, when high school players all across the country sign their college scholarships, was only two months away—on February 7—and players typically make known the schools they plan to sign with before then. That meant we didn't have much time to put together our first recruiting class, so we had to be efficient.

Outside Iowa, where we were busy trying to meet—and in some cases, locate—the coaches, we developed a one-flight recruiting plan. We laid a map on a table in our meeting room and picked out the cities that had direct flights from nearby Des Moines. We didn't have time to send coaches on trips that required connecting flights, and we didn't want recruits to have to make connecting flights every time they went home. Our itineraries consisted of one flight and a rental car. That was it.

We received positive reactions on the recruiting trails, especially in Iowa. There are some top-notch coaches in Iowa who are in it for all the right reasons. Many of them aren't full-time, paid coaches; they coach simply because they love kids and football. There seemed to be a measure of intrigue that Iowa State had hired a coach from Texas who had won a national championship. Our favorable reception in Iowa, together with my connections in Texas and Florida, made for a good combination.

It's not until a head coach is able to recruit for a full year that he can truly begin to put his stamp on a program through the players he brings in, but we did manage to get a start in the right direction during our two-month dash to National Signing Day. Plus, we began to develop contacts in Iowa, even learning how and when to reach some of the state's high school coaches.

For that first class, though, our connections and lack of connections were obvious: we signed nine players from Texas, five from Florida, and only two from Iowa. And because of the short time we had to recruit and the number of holes we had to promptly fill, twelve of the twenty-five players we signed came from junior colleges.

OUR FIRST CONTROVERSY

It wasn't long after Signing Day when our first great controversy peaked.

From the very beginning, during my interviews with Iowa State, I had made it clear that one of my first priorities would be to create a position for a chaplain in the football program. Jamie Pollard, the athletic director, had agreed to that, and now we were working on making it happen. The media got wind of the chaplaincy plan at a big Fellowship of Christian Athletes banquet in Des Moines, and almost before we knew what was happening, we found ourselves embroiled in a fierce battle.

Stirred up by the media's reports and criticisms of our plan, more than one hundred of the school's faculty members signed a petition against the addition of a chaplain, claiming that a chaplain at a state-funded institution would violate separation of church and state. They also asserted that our chaplain would favor Christianity over other faiths. The American Civil Liberties Union joined the faculty members' cause.

What made things especially frustrating for me was that the objections against the plan were unfounded. From my perspective, the chaplain would be a spiritual resource, much as student-athletes are provided tutors for their coursework or mentors for their transition into college life. The chaplain would be available to anyone who wanted to take advantage of such a resource. There would be no pressure, no coercion, and no favoritism shown to those who took part in the program. We were even setting up the position to be funded through private donations with support from the Fellowship of Christian Athletes. This was so important to Jonna and me that we joined the numerous individuals who pledged financial support. Not one cent from the school or the state would go toward having a chaplain.

Jamie cannot receive enough credit for standing strong despite the relentless opposition he faced. He publicly justified the proposal, saying that with all the pressure student-athletes were up against, they would benefit from having ready access to spiritual guidance. On one occasion during this time, the landscaping at Jamie's home was damaged. Another time trash was dumped on his lawn. Yet Jamie had said in our first interview that he would back the idea of a chaplain and that he believed it was a much-needed resource, and he remained steadfast in his support.

We use the expression "take one for the team" in sports when someone accepts the fall for the good of a group. That's exactly what happened in this case. By design, Jamie bore the brunt of the backlash. Supporters of the chaplaincy developed a strategy for facing the criticism, and Jamie became our out-front person on the issue, meaning he was the one who dealt with the media and served as our public voice. Jamie willingly took on that task, and he was strong enough to carry it out. I know it wasn't easy for him, especially with all the criticism coming from within the school, but he handled that less-than-desirable role admirably.

Despite the fierce opposition, early in the summer, university president Gregory Geoffroy approved the creation of a "life skills assistant" position for the program. It didn't matter to me what it was called. They could have called the position "rocking chair" or something goofy like that, for all I cared. The life skills assistant was everything we had intended the chaplain to be. It's just that the title *chaplain* had, for some reason, given opponents an unrealistic idea about what that person would be and do for our team. The title changed from our original plan, but the job description and the reason for it never did.

President Geoffroy stipulated that the life skills assistant would receive no funding from the school, that athletes could not be required to take part in any religious activities, and that the position would be subject to a review and reevaluation—stipulations that fit into the vision we had intended all along. We were grateful things were finally moving forward. I wouldn't say the opposition ever fully went away while I was there, but it did calm down after the president's decision. I think the unified front the detractors saw from the staff and the administration contributed to that. Jamie and President Geoffroy had given me their word that they'd support having a team chaplain, and they stuck to it.

Kevin Lykins had been the strength and conditioning coach at Stephen F. Austin when I was there, and he had since become a Baptist minister. Once we got approval for the position, I asked Kevin to come to Ames as our chaplain. I am happy to report that he is still a volunteer staff member at Iowa State and FCA's representative on campus. My dream of having a chaplain for the team required a more intense battle than I'd anticipated, but I was glad to have Kevin there to fill that role. Iowa State now had its own Chette Williams.

TAKING THE FIELD

With that controversy behind us, I was especially ready to start
the football season. Our fans were apparently ready too, as we
broke the school record for season tickets sold with more than
thirty-six thousand.

Our first game was scheduled for a Thursday night. It would
be our only non-Saturday game of the season, and playing on
a weeknight added to the electricity that always comes with a
season opener. Students get especially excited about weeknight
games because they have all day on campus to get fired up.
Fraternities and sororities plan extra activities for weeknight
games to help create a more festive atmosphere. For coaches and
players, a Thursday game puts you in more of a spotlight. With
the majority of games on Saturdays, your game receives more
attention when you play during the week. Add in all the new
elements in our program, and we got a really exciting buildup to
our season opener.

When reporters asked during the week how I felt heading into
my first game as a head coach, I compared my excitement to the
2006 Rose Bowl game, when our Longhorns beat Southern Cal
to win the national championship. That's how pumped up I was.

But I also issued a bit of a warning to our fans through the
media. I wanted them to know that our first game would be filled
with good, bad, and ugly. A major transition period comes anytime there's a change in coaching staff. Some players are bound
to transfer elsewhere, and this case was no exception. Coach
McCarney had been popular at Iowa State, and some players
were upset that the coach who had recruited them was, by all
indications, forced to resign.

In total, we had only ten of twenty-two starters returning on offense and defense combined. We would have seven new starters on offense, including players at key positions. Not only that, but we were starting from a bit of a deficit. The previous year's offense had ranked eighty-first in the nation statistically out of 119 teams in the NCAA Football Bowl Subdivision (formerly known as Division I-A). We had six players back from a defense that had ranked 102nd overall and was dead last in opponent completion percentage (72 percent). So we had our work cut out for us on both sides of the ball.

In case my warning was not enough for our fans, almost all the pollsters had picked us to finish last in the six-team North Division of the Big 12.

A solid crowd of 47,313 showed up at our Jack Trice Stadium for the first game, and as promised, we delivered a mix of good, bad, and ugly. We led Kent State 14–9 late in the third quarter, but in a span of barely two and a half minutes, Kent State scored a touchdown to take the lead, intercepted a pass, and scored another touchdown. Just like that, our lead had become a 23–14 deficit, and that was the score when the game ended.

It wasn't the start to the season we'd been hoping for, but with so many new variables in the program—new coaches, new system, new players—I suppose it wasn't altogether unexpected.

To lose our next game, though, was unexpected. And a bit demoralizing.

Northern Iowa was a member of the Football Championship Subdivision (the old Division I-AA) and wound up having an outstanding season, becoming the number one team in the FCS national rankings before losing in the second round of the play-offs and finishing with a 12–1 record.

Northern Iowa beat us 24–13, playing well and deserving to

win. It was a difficult loss for us, especially considering Iowa State had defeated Northern Iowa five consecutive times since 1994. Our guys played hard to the end, and I was encouraged by that, but a record crowd of 56,795 was on hand to see us upset by an in-state school in our own stadium. That was the season several FCS teams pulled off surprising wins over FBS teams, including what is one of college football's all-time biggest upsets— Appalachian State's victory against then-fifth-ranked Michigan. But we did not enjoy being on that list of bigger programs to lose to smaller programs.

"SHAGGY" COMES THROUGH

We were 0–2 and had not played to our potential in either game. But the schedule was kind to us in that our next game was against our archrival, the University of Iowa. Whether a team is 0–2 or 2–0, there is little a coach needs to say to his team the week it plays its biggest rival.

Iowa had won its first two games and came into our stadium favored to win by seventeen points. But those odds didn't take into account our players' never-quit mentality. Besides, we knew what was on the line in this game: the Cy-Hawk Trophy, which goes to the winner of each year's Iowa State–Iowa game. We were ready.

We led 12–0 at halftime and held on to the lead until the Hawkeyes kicked a field goal with less than four minutes remaining, giving them a 13–12 advantage. Our guys were resilient, though, and the offense drove downfield to set up a potentially game-winning twenty-eight-yard field goal with five seconds to play.

Iowa called a time-out to try to ice our kicker, Bret Culbertson, commonly known as Shaggy because of his resemblance to the cartoon character from *Scooby-Doo*. Bret was a senior and a good kicker, but he had missed a few critical field goals during his career. And like the rest of the team, he was off to a slow start that season, missing all three of his field goal attempts prior to this game.

During the time-out, I pulled Bret aside. "Visualize and kick it," I told him. That's just what he did, nailing the kick and bringing the score to 15–13.

Only one second remained on the clock, but fittingly for the start of our season, not even the final second would expire without a fight. We kicked off, and Iowa's return man added drama to the finish that we didn't really need, taking the ball sixty-five yards, all the way back to our twenty-five yard line, before Michael Bibbs tackled him to end the game.

We won 15–13, with Bret having accounted for all of our points with a school record–tying five field goals. When the final tackle was made, Bret sprinted to the Iowa sideline and grabbed the coveted Cy-Hawk Trophy. We had earned it back from Iowa.

Shaggy's teammates hoisted their hero onto their shoulders, and our fans stormed the field to celebrate the victory. With thousands of cheering people on the field, Bret was unable to locate his wife, Kristina, who was expecting the couple's first child the next spring. I can still see the tears of joy in Bret's eyes at the postgame press conference as he described the feeling of making the winning kick. Then he excused himself to find his wife and share his excitement with her.

That was truly a moment. College football is a big business now, but it's still a game, and it's still played and coached by people who experience a wide range of human emotions. Knowing that Bret had endured criticism in his career before we arrived and then having gotten acquainted with him as simply a great kid with a sweet and tender nature, I was elated for him that day. And for our team, too. I was presented with the game ball for my first victory as head coach, and while I would rather have had the Iowa game be my third victory instead of my first, it was certainly a victory to remember.

THROUGH CHILDREN'S EYES

After defeating Iowa, we suffered a true heartbreaker at Toledo, 36–35. It was a back-and-forth game until we took a 35–24 lead with less than six minutes left in the game. Then our special teams fell apart. Toledo returned our kickoff for a touchdown to make the score 35–30. We missed three or four tackles on the return, and that touchdown ended up changing the game entirely. When we got the ball back, we weren't able to pick up a first down, and we sent our punt team onto the field. But the snap got past our punter and rolled into the end zone, where Toledo recovered for a touchdown and a 36–35 lead. On the ensuing kickoff, one of our defensive backs gave us a good return before being stopped just short of midfield. From there, we took the ball to Toledo's twenty-one yard line, setting up a game-winning thirty-eight-yard field goal attempt for Bret Culbertson. But with eleven seconds on the clock, Bret's kick was partially blocked and went wide left of the goalpost.

That's the kind of game that rips at your gut. While the Toledo players celebrated their dynamic comeback, our players' faces were marked by pain as they left the field. Our guys knew we had given away a victory. That was our last nonconference game, and we should have been 2–2 starting conference play. Instead, we were 1–3. There's only a one-game difference between those two records, but a lot of emotion is packed into those little numbers. Especially when the fourth game that made us 1–3 was a loss like the one against Toledo.

Our conference schedule began with a tough chore: playing at Nebraska. The Cornhuskers are one of the nation's most storied college football programs. When you play at Nebraska, you can count on two things. First, Nebraska will play a great game because they always do at home. Second, there will be eighty thousand-plus Cornhuskers fans wearing red and cheering loudly for their team. Nebraska has some of college football's most ardent supporters. They say that on a Nebraska game day, Memorial Stadium is essentially the third-largest city in Nebraska. It is an incredibly difficult place for visiting teams to play.

Each Friday night before a Saturday game, I always call home and talk to my family. It's one of our rituals I wouldn't dare miss. When I called home on the eve of our first conference road game, I talked to Jonna first, then the kids.

"Just talk to me, baby," I said to Landry. "It's Friday night before the game and Dad's a little nervous."

"You're going to do great," Landry said. "I've been to practice this week, and you're going to do good."

Landry handed the phone to my boy, Cally.

"Tell me something good," I said to Cally.

"I've seen your practices this week," he said. "You've coached 'em good. It's gonna be all right."

Kennedy was next.

"I'm nervous," I told her. "Give me some good news. I'm looking for some encouragement."

"Hey, Dad, don't worry about a thing," she said in her cheerful voice. "You've got a six-year contract."

BUILDING A PROGRAM

Nebraska beat us 35–17, and that set us out on an 0–5 start in conference play. The third conference game was a 56–3 loss at home to twenty-second-ranked Texas, against my old boss, Mack Brown. That was one of the roughest games I've endured as a head coach.

It was one of those miserable days a team runs into sometimes where nothing goes right, and Mack's team probably could have scored a hundred points against us. But Mack demonstrated his class, as usual. Mack had his team run the ball straight into our defense for most of the fourth quarter to keep the clock moving and, thus, to keep down the score. Our crowd began thinning out early in the second half. By the end of the game, only the most die-hard of our die-hard fans were still around. Who could blame those who left early? It was the largest margin in a home loss for Iowa State in twenty years, and believe me, the final score could have been even uglier than the 56–3 tally.

I was with Mack for only two years at Texas, but he was—and still is—a role model to me. I called on Mack for advice when I was a new head coach, and I continue to do so. In addition to sharing his football expertise, Mack has provided wise counsel regarding issues I've had to learn how to handle as a head coach. For example, when I have been confronted with discipline problems that have made it into the public arena, Mack has been a trusted sounding board, willing to talk with me at any time. Every new head coach needs an experienced coach like Mack to be able to call upon for guidance.

At Texas, I watched how Mack took football and his role as coach seriously, but how he also saw the value in making sure his players were having fun. There is so much pressure and so much money involved in college football nowadays, and winning can become practically an obsession. Mack emphasized that players need to have fun with football. "After all," he would remind his coaching staff, "the players are still kids." As I continued to make mental notes for what I would do when I ran my own program, I made sure to add Mack's philosophy of keeping the joy in the sport.

Mack also taught me the importance of including coaches' wives as part of the football program and having the wives involved in the players' lives. The reality is that many of our players come from single-parent homes, and as they grew up, Mom was the only one raising them. Then, when they left home for college, it was a big adjustment for them to be away from their mothers. From Mack, I learned what an important mothering role coaches' wives can fill for players, and that is now a staple of our program too.

Our off-the-field relationship aside, 56–3 was a difficult pill to swallow.

TV cameras were pretty much on top of Mack and me when we met at midfield after the game. As we shook hands, Mack didn't say the usual "Good game." Instead, he grabbed the back of my head with his left hand and pulled it toward him, where he could talk into my ear so no one else could hear what he was saying.

"There was nothing I enjoyed about this game," he told me. Then he added that he loved me.

It was a special, personal moment coming from someone I respected and had learned so much from in only two seasons.

I was also able to meet up with some of my former Longhorns players on the field after the game. Many hugged me and told me they missed me. I missed them, too, and I realized just how much that was true during the course of the game.

Well after the game, Mack's wife, Sally, came over to our athletic offices at the stadium and gathered our coaches' wives together. Sally offered encouraging words to the wives, giving them a boost before they headed home to be with their husbands, who had just suffered a humiliating day at the office. That's Mack and Sally for you—classy people at all times.

Aside from those few shining postgame moments, what I remember most about that day is an awful, almost-sick feeling in my stomach as the game played out. Texas teams go into every game not just knowing they can win, but expecting to win. Our guys weren't there yet. I was seven games into my head coaching career, and we had won only once. It felt different on our sideline than it had during those two years on the Texas sideline. Our Iowa State players had yet to develop that expect-to-win attitude. It's a different mentality, and it typically produces different results. That day, it struck me how much I missed that feeling of expecting to win every week.

The following Monday, Mack and I talked on the phone. He gave me a rundown of what his coaches had observed about us when looking at game film before we played. He offered evaluations of some of the guys he considered to be our better players. Before we hung up, Mack told me, "You're doing it right. Just stay with it. The kids are playing hard. They're not giving up."

In the face of such a rocky start, when we weren't seeing the results we wanted, that was just the boost I needed to keep pressing on—and to motivate my players to do the same. After the Texas loss, with our record at 1–6 and five games remaining, I told our guys that they couldn't change the beginning of the season, but they could begin to change the end.

The next two games, though they were both losses, supported

what Mack had said about our kids not giving up. Oklahoma came to Ames for our homecoming game as the fourth-ranked team in the country. I could see in our kids' eyes that they didn't think they could beat Oklahoma, but they went out on that field and played with everything they had. Our defense forced a turnover in the first quarter that we converted into a touchdown. We had chances to add to our lead, but we missed a field goal and failed to convert a fourth and one deep in OU's territory. Still, though, we led the number four team in the country 7–0 at halftime.

Oklahoma came back in the second half with two touchdowns and led 14–7 early in the fourth quarter. We drove into Oklahoma's end of the field and looked like we were headed for a touchdown. No one but our coaching staff knew this, but if we had scored a touchdown there, we planned to go for a two-point conversion to take a one-point lead instead of kicking the extra point to tie the score at fourteen. We had a two-point play that we were confident would work against Oklahoma's defense. We didn't get a chance to use that play, though, because, again, we missed another scoring chance when we threw an interception in the end zone. It took a late field goal for Oklahoma to put us away and win 17–7.

The following week we traveled to thirteenth-ranked Missouri. We fell behind 14–0 midway through the first quarter, but our kids hung in there and we got to within three points of Missouri in the second quarter. We were within one or two touchdowns for most of the second half until Missouri scored a touchdown in the fourth quarter to put them up by twenty-one points. They eventually beat us 42–28. We made major mistakes in both the Oklahoma and Missouri games, but knowing we had opportunities to beat two highly ranked teams built confidence in our players.

We followed those losses with two big home victories—big since they were both conference games—against Kansas State (31–20) and Colorado (31–28).

On the field before the Kansas State game, I walked over to shake hands with their coach, Ron Prince. Ron was in his second season as head coach, so the memory of being a first-year coach remained fresh for him.

"Gene," he told me, "I know it's tough. Stick to what you believe in, and don't deviate off that path. You were a great defensive coordinator, and you'll be a great head coach."

His encouragement not to deviate from what I believed in was exactly what I needed to hear, and I'll always be grateful to Ron for his reassurance that day.

After beating Kansas State and Colorado, we ended our season on a downer, a 45–7 loss at fourth-ranked Kansas that left us with a 3–9 record. We ended up fifth in the Big 12 North, tied with Nebraska at 2–6.

It wasn't the type of record we had hoped for, but I felt confident we had something to build on. The players had worked hard and believed in our program, and they were already beginning to understand what it felt like to compete with the teams on our schedule. We were progressing to the point of believing that we had a chance to win every week. Next we needed to believe that we *would* win.

Although we had only those three victories, they were solid victories that could serve as a starting place for the next season. Beating Iowa was huge for our fans and for in-state recruiting. Iowa was more talented than we were, but our kids had learned to overcome that by fighting for the entire game. Winning back-to-back conference games near the end of the season—especially coming off a long losing streak—gave us momentum as we looked ahead to next year and as we recruited high school players.

It was true that at 3–9 we had won one fewer game than the previous year's team—and records are the bottom line by which coaches are judged. Still, I believed we had improved in some key areas that first season. We certainly had our share of frustrating moments, but by winning two of our final three games, we were able to end on an up note. The foundation of our program was coming together.

The hardest thing about my first season as a head coach was figuring out how to divide my time among the offense, the defense, and the special teams. I had hired coordinators for each unit who I was confident could do the job—guys I knew I could trust. Their roles were clear, but I wasn't sure exactly what my role was with the team.

I wanted to spend time with the defense because I had been a defensive coordinator for a long time and I was confident in my abilities to help a defense. But I also felt I needed to be involved with the offense since I knew what an offense could do to hurt a defense. And a head coach *always* worries about special teams, so I felt a pull to spend time in that area. I spent a lot of time that first season trying to decide where I needed to be and how I could best help my coordinators.

Although each coordinator was in charge of his unit, as head coach I was ultimately responsible for whether we won or lost. Yet I wasn't actually in control of the offense, the defense, or the special teams. The coordinators were. The bottom line, I felt, was that I was responsible without being in control. The struggle over trying to define my role as head coach put more stress on me than I had ever experienced as a defensive coordinator. Plus, as the head coach, I was responsible for disciplining players and monitoring grades and class attendance so we wouldn't lose any players for academic reasons. That was a challenge I could only learn to deal with as the season progressed, and by the end of the season, I still didn't feel like I had a good handle on it.

After our final game, I called in a couple of seniors—wide receiver Todd Blythe and quarterback Bret Meyer. I am always questioning players about how to improve our program, and I specifically sought out Todd's and Bret's thoughts because of how long they had been with the Cyclones and because of their leadership roles on the team. Besides, you can usually count on good, honest evaluations from outgoing seniors who no longer have to be concerned about how their feedback could affect their playing time.

I heard what I had hoped—and needed—to hear. Both players gave a big thumbs-up to what we were doing with the program. They both acknowledged our team's struggles in my first season, but they added that they believed we were headed in the right direction. They said that the coaching staff was doing a great job and that they had observed a noticeable upgrade in the types of recruits who were coming in for visits. Their feedback was an affirmation to me: *Keep doing what you're doing to get this program turned around. We're getting there. Keep going in that direction.*

We had carried some momentum into our off-season by the way we finished the season, and I had heard from team leaders that the players supported what we were doing and believed our team would turn around soon. We had much to look forward to in 2008.

3

....

LESSONS IN LOSSES

AS COLD AS the weather was in Iowa, the people were equally warm.

Many of the fans we came into contact with from across the state boasted a long history of agriculture and heartland values. What some of them lacked in financial means they more than made up for with wealth of another sort: family heritage and a strong work ethic.

We had the opportunity to meet people who farmed hundreds of acres—families who for generations had lived and died on the land they worked, families whose children woke up at 4:30 a.m. to do their chores. These people worked hard, and they expected nothing more from life than what the good Lord and their land provided.

As a general rule, college football can be a playground for

big-money alumni. It's nothing out of the ordinary for an alum to ask the coach if he wants to fly on his personal jet or to invite him to stay at his multimillion-dollar beach house. Iowa State was no exception in that respect. But in addition to the private jets and enticing getaways, there was also a sense of family and community you might not expect elsewhere. Someone might walk up to you at a home game and say, "Here's ten slabs of ribs." Or they'd offer to cook dinner for you and the team. Some would show up with a cooler filled with pork and their special barbecue sauce made from secret family recipes. It probably could go without saying, but there was plenty of corn on the cob, too. It was refreshing for Jonna and me to be around down-to-earth, as-good-as-they-come people like that. We recognized that we were raising our family among people who lived out the values our country was built upon.

There was one woman who would send me letters almost daily, reminding me that she was praying for me and expressing appreciation for the times she heard me on television talking about the high standards we expected from our players or mentioning my faith. During football season she would write that she would love to come to an Iowa State game, but she was on her combine out in the fields and couldn't make it to Ames.

If it hadn't been for the warmhearted people, I don't know how we'd have made it through those Iowa winters. Jonna and I grew up in Florida. I graduated from the University of Florida, and she graduated from Florida State University. After that I coached high school football in Florida, and my college coaching career took me to South Carolina, Tennessee, Texas, Florida, Alabama, and then back to Texas. In case you missed the trend there, those states are all decidedly south of Iowa. And decidedly warmer.

One of my first days in Ames, after Jonna and the kids had returned to Texas to finish everything up at school and at home, the digital temperature gauge in my car read below zero. I watched the temperature climb until it reached zero, then a one without a minus sign in front of it. "Yes!" I exclaimed. I remember driving down the road thinking, *How messed up is it that I'm excited because it's one degree?*

I added to my vocabulary *whiteout* (when the ground and air are so white with snow that it's difficult to see anything) and *black ice* (a practically invisible sheet of ice on a road that can cause your car to unexpectedly begin spinning). I learned to allow the oil in my car to warm and thin before driving. I also discovered the importance of owning a full-length coat rather than the waist-length coats I was accustomed to wearing during Southern "winters."

The first time my family experienced really cold weather after moving to Ames, the biting wind informed Jonna that her old wardrobe wasn't going to cut it there. She quickly learned that if you're wearing jeans in a bitter wind, you wouldn't have been much worse off in a pair of shorts. Jonna is a thrifty shopper, but this was a nonnegotiable for my new salary: it was time to buy entirely new sets of winter clothes for her and the kids.

The weather was certainly an adjustment, but it gave us more family time inside our home. It also created outdoor opportunities we'd never had. We held highly competitive family snowball fights, and we enjoyed wrestling in the snow and going sledding. Then there was one of our crazier games: on extra-cold, windy, and snowy days, the kids and I would put on our bathing suits and see who could stay outside the longest before quitting and going back inside. For some reason I can't recall, the rules of our game allowed us to wear stocking caps, as if keeping our heads and ears covered while practically the rest of our bodies were exposed was going to prevent us from catching pneumonia.

It was a big change, to be sure. But we were having a good time living in Ames.

NEW LOOK, DIFFERENT RESULTS?

As my second season with the Cyclones ramped up, we were continuing to adjust to some major changes on the team, and I believed we were poised to make the most of them.

Going from my first season to my second, we lost only four starters on offense and four on defense, but we did need to replace some key playmakers on both sides. We had brought in a strong recruiting class with twenty-five signees, including fourteen total players from Florida (nine) and Texas (five). We signed four players from Iowa high schools, and only one of our signees came from a junior college.

Going into our first season, we had had to make a fundamental decision: should we play the older guys or the younger guys? We determined that we would play our seniors as much as we could. They had put three or four years into the Iowa State football program, and they'd had some success before losing the head coach who had recruited them. Then, when I arrived, they had stayed aboard despite my high expectations, most of them knowing this would be their final season of playing football anywhere. Those guys had earned their playing time, so we started and leaned heavily on the older players as much as possible. But for our second season, we were going young. By playing the older guys the previous year, we had been able to redshirt some of the freshmen we had brought in with our first recruiting class.

The redshirts were able to go through a season of our program without playing; thus, they still had four years of eligibility left. So we pretty much had a small group of experienced freshmen, if you will, to mix in with the talented freshmen from our first full recruiting class. Going young at as many positions as possible was the best route for our long-range plan for making Iowa State a winning program.

Besides our different approach for our second season, we looked different too. I wanted to change as much about the program as I could, including what we wore. We asked our fans to help us select new uniforms and helmets, and more than thirty-five thousand voted for their choices on our athletic department website. Our marketing team conducted a great deal of research, and we brought our uniform maker, Nike, into the discussions too. This wasn't simply *Let's try something different.* We wanted to *be* different.

For the matchup against the Hawkeyes my first season, we had worn a throwback uniform to honor coach Earle Bruce's Iowa State team that had played in the 1977 Peach Bowl (now the Chick-fil-A Bowl). The uniforms were a big hit with our fans and players, and I liked them a lot myself. The result of our new uniform search was a throwback-style jersey in our deep cardinal and gold, similar to what we had worn against Iowa. We were one of two BCS schools I knew of that had cardinal and gold as primary colors, and over the years the cardinal red had moved more toward a bright red. We wanted to get back to our true colors.

Our helmets changed, too, with the popular "Cy" logo giving way to a cardinal *I* with a gold *STATE* superimposed on it. We even changed our face masks to old-school gray instead of white or a school color, like most teams go with. We thought the gray face masks added an element of toughness. Our goal was to have even the smallest uniform detail symbolize that we were doing things completely different for our second season.

Jack Trice Stadium also had a new look after receiving a $19.5 million update. Suites had been added, club levels had been renovated, and amenities for fans had been significantly upgraded.

The uniforms looked better, the stadium looked better, and on the field, we were looking better too. We were desperate to avoid the slow start we'd suffered our first season, and we did. Instead of opening with two losses, we started the 2008 season 2–0.

The season opener was another Thursday night home game, this time against FCS school South Dakota State. We had our sloppy moments, but we forced six turnovers and won easily, 44–17. The next week Kent State came calling again, and we made up for the previous season's loss to the Golden Flashes, winning 48–28.

We played like a young team in the two victories, but there were promising signs. More important, we were 2–0, and regardless of how you get there, being 2–0 is better than the other possibilities.

Next on the schedule was our big game with Iowa for the Cy-Hawk Trophy. Iowa had also won its first two games, and with both teams undefeated, the anticipation was jacked even higher than usual.

The game was on Iowa's field this time, and it started out as tightly contested as you'd expect for a rivalry game. Heading into the fourth quarter, the score was tied 3–3. Then Iowa scored two touchdowns, including one on a game-clinching punt return. We'd had plenty of opportunities to take control of the game, but we threw three interceptions, missed three field goals, and failed to score three times after driving the ball to Iowa's red zone. They ended up defeating us 17–5 to reclaim the Cy-Hawk Trophy.

Missed opportunities became a theme for the rest of the season. The Iowa loss started a ten-game losing streak, and we finished 2–10 overall and 0–8 in the Big 12.

In our first game after losing to Iowa, we trailed by twenty-one points at the University of Nevada, Las Vegas, before coming back to tie the score, then lost 34–31 in overtime.

In our next game, at sixteenth-ranked Kansas, we led 20–0 at halftime. Then the Jayhawks showed why they were a nationally ranked team, rallying to take a 35–26 lead with about three and a half minutes left. We scored a touchdown to make it 35–33 and recovered an onside kick. On the final play of the game, we had a long pass glance off a receiver's outstretched fingertips for what could have been a prime opportunity to score a game-winning touchdown.

In our eighth game of the losing streak, we trailed at Colorado 28–24 late in the fourth quarter. We drove sixty yards to the Buffaloes' one yard line with three seconds remaining. On the final play our running back was tackled for a loss, and we suffered another heartbreaking defeat.

We'd hoped to at least end on a positive note, but in the final game of the season, at Kansas State, we lost 38–30 even though our quarterback, Austen Arnaud, passed for a school-record 440 yards. On the last play of the game and the season, Austen completed a touchdown pass to R. J. Sumrall. Afterward I told the media that our final drive and touchdown showed that our players had not quit—they'd played hard all the way to the end.

That could have been a fitting description of our entire season. We lost some close games, and we lost some not-so-close games. I would not even attempt to spin a 2–10 record into anything other than what it is. But as discouraging as our final record was, I hung on to a certain level of hope when I considered our players' attitudes and refusal to quit. I've seen teams that will pack up their tents late in the season after struggling to win. Losing close games repeatedly can add to that frustration for teams. But as the close games late in the season demonstrated, our guys were in every game to win. We just didn't do what it took to win enough times.

REDEFINING SUCCESS

The losing was hard on the players, and it was hard on me. As I reflected on other coaching experiences in my career, I realized I had won so consistently at those schools that I took winning for granted. There was one stretch when I was coaching at Auburn and Texas during which our teams won twenty-nine consecutive games. That is the equivalent of almost three full seasons without losing once.

In the nineteen seasons I had coached at the college level, whether I was a graduate assistant, assistant head coach, or some other title in between, I had been on only two teams that finished seasons with losing records. Now here I was with two losing seasons in my two years as head coach at Iowa State.

It's difficult to stand up in front of a hundred players every week and try to find a new way to spin the same old message: "We gave it all we had, but we need just a little more." At some point during a stretch of giving those speeches, you want to just shrug your shoulders and say, "I've run out of stuff to say here." But there you are each Sunday, looking your kids in the eyes and saying, "Let's go after it again."

To our players' credit, they did. They continued to practice hard and play hard. The guys were always motivated to play, and that is one thing that never wavered during my time at Iowa State. Our record was poor, but I knew that every head coach we went up against was holding his breath, realizing our guys were going to scratch and claw and battle for every game.

I had come to Iowa State with a long-range plan of tearing the program down to ground level, laying a new foundation, then building it up again. During that second season, we were beginning to do just that. Coming off a strong recruiting class, we had eleven freshmen and five redshirt freshmen who saw significant playing time. Those are high numbers. There is give-and-take involved when you play that many youngsters—you give now so you can take later. We decided to start them young because we could see their potential to mature in our system. We expected growing pains, and we knew we had to keep our sights on our long-range vision. In our third and fourth seasons, we were going to have a core of talented players who had taken some licks early in their careers but who also had been toughened and made hungry by fighting through the adversity.

We were following our plan, and our program was being built. But despite my attempt to look at the overall picture for the program, the losses of the moment were eating at me.

I dived deep into self-evaluation mode. The natural reaction when a coach loses is to evaluate and critique everything about his program. We had played so many close games that I felt like we should have won, so I tried to figure out if there was something I was doing as head coach that was preventing us from winning the tight ones. I asked myself every question I could think of in hopes of finding even one answer that would make our team better. Was there more I could have been doing to lead the team? Did I need to take more control? Did I have too much control? Was I hanging on to responsibilities I should have been allowing my assistant coaches to handle?

Because this was my first go-around as a head coach, I had no previous success in that role to draw upon. I couldn't look back on winning seasons and pinpoint what was different in this case. I didn't know what it felt like to be a winning head coach or what it took to win from the top spot in a program. I was learning how to run a program, and I was having to do so during tough times from a football standpoint. As you progress through the coaching ranks, you hear that being a head coach is much different from being an assistant coach. But until you actually make the transition, you have no idea just how big of a jump it truly is. I think even winning as an assistant coach and winning as a head coach is like comparing apples and oranges. So when I moved from being a winning assistant coach to a losing head coach, there was little from my assistant days I could tap into for help.

Here I was, finally a head coach after working hard for so long to become one, and I knew that outside our program I was being viewed as a flop. Probably even a major failure.

In the midst of this time of agonizing soul-searching, confirmation that our program was progressing came from an unexpected source: the players themselves. Several came to me at different times with what amounted to votes of confidence. They would say that while our record wasn't as good as in recent years, they felt much more positive than they had during the 4–8 season before our staff arrived. They said they recognized that we had suffered some hard knocks but that they were learning a lot and believed we were getting better. They said they loved playing football, they shared the vision for what the coaches were telling them about our program, and they were understanding more about football—and also about life.

Based on our win-loss record, it was a bleak season. But as I observed how the players were getting what we were teaching, I counted it as a victory of the non-scoreboard variety.

GOD IS BIGGER THAN 5–19

As we moved into that off-season after my second year at Iowa State, it was a tense time for me—partly because I strongly dislike losing, and also because I understood that coaches with losing records don't keep their jobs for long. Our two-season record of 5–19 loomed large over my career as head coach.

I started asking myself whether I believed that God had sent me to Iowa State to have consecutive losing seasons. Was this really what he wanted for me? One thing I knew for sure was that for my competitive nature, the losing had gotten difficult to handle week in and week out.

One night in her prayer time, Jonna felt that God was asking her some gut-wrenching questions. She wrote the questions in her journal and shared them with me:

1. Why are we coaching football?
2. If we are coaching for the purpose God has given us, would we be okay if we coached at Iowa State forever and lost more games than we won?
3. Could we put aside the world's definition of success and accept only God's definition of success?
4. Do we trust God with our lives, our family, and our job security?

As Jonna and I discussed those questions, we gradually began to experience a level of peace. We had accepted the Iowa State job because we believed without hesitation that God wanted us in Iowa. God wasn't calling us to win; he was just calling us to be obedient and faithful. So with renewed perspective, we focused on our true purpose in coaching football. It gave us comfort to know that there was a God-ordained reason for our being at Iowa State—and comfort was practically impossible to come by in that season.

But just because you have comfort, and just because you believe that God has called you to a certain place, doesn't mean you don't feel the bumps and potholes in your path. There was no getting around the fact that we had a 5–19 record in my first two seasons. It was disappointing to our players, to our school, and to our fans. But no one was more disappointed in our record than I was.

That two-year stretch of losing became another time of spiritual growth for me. Kevin Lykins, our life skills assistant (chaplain!), was with me every step of the way. Kevin held a coaches' Bible study every Thursday morning, but Tuesday mornings were a time for Kevin and me to meet alone. I looked forward to our weekly meetings, and the spiritual guidance Kevin gave me during those times served as a springboard to help me face my job challenges the rest of the week. That season we studied Nehemiah.

If you're not familiar with Nehemiah, his story is told in the Old Testament book that bears his name. Nehemiah was an officer of high rank under Artaxerxes, king of Persia, during the 400s BC. When Nehemiah learned that the walls of the city of Jerusalem, his home city, had been destroyed, he asked Artaxerxes for permission to rebuild them. With the king's permission he returned to Jerusalem and oversaw a wall-rebuilding project that, despite stiff opposition from enemies on all sides, was completed in only fifty-two days. Now that's a quick construction project.

Over the course of that study, I learned that Nehemiah was a man of purpose, courage, and action. The more I read about his leadership through times of hardship and frustration, the more timely it felt for my own rebuilding project. Each week Kevin delved into the Scripture and aptly applied lessons from Nehemiah's situation to mine. I gained strength and insight from considering how one of the greatest men of the Bible had, twenty-four hundred years earlier, faced leadership struggles similar to what I was up against.

Kevin was my guy during that time. He was my sounding board—one of the major reasons I got through as many tough times as I did. Kevin helped me to stay focused on what mattered most with a football team that was disappointed each week yet refused to quit. Kevin's encouragement and our times of study and prayer kept me going so I could continue to motivate my players during our losing streak and motivate the coaching staff to do the same. Trust me, even when you know that you have a higher purpose than football and you are working for results that don't show up on a scoreboard, it's not easy to lose week after week. It's draining, and it tears you up inside. There were games when I was standing on the sideline and the clock was counting down to another loss, and my gut would just hurt. For myself, for my coaches, for my players, for the fans.

Yet through those tough times, I grew. There is something inherent in failure that causes you to reflect on the deeper things of life in a way that winning never can. Through it all, Jonna and

I clung to the belief that if God places you somewhere and you do things the way he wants you to, his hand remains on you. Whether that means a winning record or not.

During that time, God reminded me that he'd called me to be more than a football coach. As big as 5–19 seemed, our God was bigger than that, and my security belonged in him rather than in my coaching ability or what other people thought of the job I was doing.

Jonna's four questions caused me to evaluate the word *winning*. Those outside the program said we needed to be winning games, and I agreed. But through prayer, I sensed this reminder: "You came here for a reason. You're winning lives. You're winning kids over. You're winning with what you have put in place in this program. You're doing a different kind of winning."

I couldn't escape that question: *If we are coaching for the purpose God has given us, would we be okay if we coached at Iowa State forever and lost more games than we won every year?*

We weren't winning on the field, but we were winning in other ways. We were winning in the way that we believed God wanted us to win. My problem was that I was used to winning on the field, and that wasn't happening. It was a big-time ego check for me.

If we had sensed God asking that question while we were at Texas or Auburn, our answer would have been, "Absolutely. We are going to serve you no matter what." But being in the context of so much on-field winning at those schools would have clouded our answer. Now I really needed to rely on God rather than my own coaching abilities. I needed to be asked that question when I was 5–19.

The message of 5–19 became personal for Jonna and me. "We serve a God who is bigger than 5–19" became a refrain of sorts for us, a constant reminder that God had brought us to Iowa State and that he remained in charge of our journey.

We didn't see a destination on our journey beyond Iowa State. We planned on being there awhile longer, and all our coaches were working their tails off for our long-range plan. We were at Iowa State to do the best we could there, and if a call came for another opportunity, we would deal with that when it happened.

That call came sooner than we ever imagined.

4

....

A "GOD THING"

WHEN YOU HAVE a poor record, you can count on speculation that your job is in jeopardy. I make it a point to never read or listen to what the media are saying about my program. There are people within the athletic department who keep me apprised of any negative or potentially damaging reports I need to be aware of as the head coach, but I don't subscribe to newspapers and I don't listen to radio or television commentaries about my program.

I appreciate the media and the job they have to do, but I choose not to receive any validation from what the media broadcasts or prints. I'll tell you a little later about the circle we have at Auburn and how we try to block out the criticisms of those outside the core group of people whose opinions matter to us.

Our beat writers are extremely fair, and I respect their job and what it entails. I have good working relationships with the reporters who are around our team on a daily basis, but for me it is strictly a professional relationship.

What is frustrating is that many stories are nothing more than speculation to begin with, reported by people who don't have access to all the facts. Internet message boards and fan sites have become extremely popular, especially in college sports, but too often those become nothing more than places for people to post uninformed judgments. It's sad that some of these opinion shapers are heard by so many people even though their perspectives are not based on facts.

Behind the scenes and, thus, going unreported was the fact that Jamie Pollard, our athletic director, had informed me before our season ended that he wanted to extend my contract. He was pleased with the program's direction and told me he essentially wanted to pretend the first two years of my contract had never happened. Jamie's proposal was to extend my contract so it would run six more years instead of the four years that remained on the initial agreement. It provided me with a sense of security and affirmation—both personally and professionally—to know that my boss liked where we were headed and believed we were doing the right things to take the program where he had hired me to take it. The extension was almost finalized and we were close to signing the new contract when something unexpected happened.

I had been on the road recruiting, and shortly after I returned home, my phone rang. It was Jamie, telling me he had received a call that he'd expected to get but had hoped would come later rather than sooner.

"Who was it?" I asked.

"It was Jay Jacobs," he replied. Jay had worked in the Auburn athletic department when I was there, and he had been promoted to athletic director shortly before I left for Texas.

"About what?" I asked. I had no clue why Jay would be talking to Jamie.

"About their head coaching job," Jamie replied.

Tommy Tuberville, the head coach during my three seasons at Auburn, had resigned less than a week after the regular season ended. Tommy had been at Auburn for ten seasons and had a solid 85–40 record there. But Auburn had gone 5–7 in 2008, lost six of its final seven games, and was defeated 36–0 by Alabama on national television in the final game.

Ever since my first tenure at Auburn, it had been my dream to be head coach there. Jonna and I loved Auburn University and the city of Auburn. The city's school system is great, and the people are Southern friendly. And I've never encountered a program with more passion, energy, and tradition.

The two words that most often come to mind when I'm asked to describe Auburn University are *allegiance* and *conviction*. Auburn people have a deep loyalty to and a strong belief in their school, and that's what really separates Auburn from other universities. I'm big on allegiance because I think we all have an inner desire to be devoted to someone or something.

If you have some extra time in an airport and you see someone walk past with *Auburn* or the interlocking *AU* on his or her clothing, follow that person and see how many times a total stranger will shout, "War Eagle!"—the school's battle cry—to him or her. I often say that our alums didn't *go* to Auburn—they *are* Auburn. They will tell you the same thing, and you'll notice the allegiance and conviction in their voices when they say it.

This rich Auburn heritage comes together with a fury on game day. Auburn's Jordan-Hare Stadium seats eighty-eight thousand. To put that in perspective, the city's population is only about fifty thousand, and the school's enrollment is twenty-five thousand. People from all over Alabama and throughout the Southeast drive into Auburn for football games. Every game day is a major event.

And then there's the Tiger Walk. If you're a sports fan and haven't witnessed it yet, you should add it to your bucket list. A number of other schools have similar traditions, but none can duplicate the passion of Auburn fans. In a tradition that dates to the 1960s, Auburn players and coaches are bused from the team hotel to the stadium two hours before kickoff. But instead of being dropped off right outside the locker room, the buses stop short of the stadium and the players walk through a throng of thousands of screaming, shoulder-slapping, sign-waving fans who line South Donahue Drive leading to the stadium. When I say thousands, that is no exaggeration. Tiger Walk for a game against Alabama will attract almost twenty thousand fans. It's an awesome scene—everywhere you look, there are painted faces and chests, waving pom-poms, and orange and blue shirts. It's common to spot three generations of Auburn fans together in the crowd.

As we get closer to the stadium, the path through the fans gets so narrow that we have to pass through single file. Seeing the turnout for the Tiger Walk and feeling the fans' energy puts goose bumps on top of your goose bumps. I'll pass through the crowd in my suit, pumping my fists and waving my arms to the fans. By the time I finish Tiger Walk, I am drenched in sweat. I feel like I've just finished playing four quarters of football.

We've also added Tiger Walks as part of the routine before

some road games, with Auburn fans showing up early to greet and cheer their team into the opposing team's stadium. We'll have as many as five thousand fans at a Tiger Walk for a road game.

I remember one Tiger Walk in particular. It was in 2002, my first season as a defensive coordinator at Auburn, before our game at Alabama. A man who had to be seventy-five or eighty years old grabbed me by my jacket. There were tears on his face. "Coach," he said, "you've got to kick their [you-know-what]. This is the game of our lives." He kept hold of my jacket and wouldn't let me go. Alabama was 9–2 and had beaten LSU 31–0 the week before. They were favored to beat us, and their offense was really good. "You've gotta stop them," the fan pretty much commanded me. That's how emotional Tiger Walks can become.

As kickoff nears, the school's "War Eagle" makes a live flight into the stadium. Auburn has three eagles (Tiger, Nova, and Spirit) that represent the school. (Here's a piece of trivia for you: one of the eagles took part in the opening ceremonies for the 2002 Winter Olympics in Salt Lake City.) Before every game, the Auburn fans stand, wave orange and blue pom-poms or towels, and cheer as one of the eagles circles the field a few times. Fans chant, "Waaaaarrrrrrr!" throughout the entire flight. When the eagle lands at midfield, they chant, "Eagle! Hey!" in unison. The coaches and players miss out on the flight because it takes place while they're in the locker room, but it has to be one of the most awe-inspiring scenes in all of college football. If you can't watch the Tiger Walk and the eagle flight in person, I'd recommend you find them on YouTube. It's nothing like witnessing these traditions in person, but it will give you a sense of the game day atmosphere at Auburn.

Another Auburn tradition is Toomer's Corner—where the

campus and city meet at the intersection of College Street and Magnolia Avenue. For many years Toomer's Corner has been the gathering place for athletic celebrations. After every football win, as well as for notable wins in other sports, Auburn students and residents come together and "roll" the trees at Toomer's Corner with toilet paper. Celebrations go on for hours, and at the end, all the tissue leaves a snowlike blanket for some poor souls to clean up.

After we left Auburn for Texas following the 2004 season, we always said that Auburn would be the one university we would pick for our kids to attend if we had a choice. The world of coaching is so transient, and when you find a place that is a good fit for your family, your lifestyle, and your values, you want to be there . . . and stay put. That's what Auburn became for us: a place I could envision returning to as head coach and remaining until I retired.

Despite my dream of coaching at Auburn one day, when I heard that Tommy had stepped down, the thought of going back didn't last any longer than the snap of a finger. I knew that with a 5–19 record I was not hirable at Auburn. I mean, this was *Auburn*. Auburn is one of the top jobs in the country. It's a place that hires head coaches who have won, and sometimes for long periods of time. As a general rule, Auburn can hire anyone it wants to, and I'm sure most coaches would crawl to Auburn for a chance at the job. In my mind, it wasn't in the realm of possibility for the university to even entertain the idea of looking at a coach who was 5–19.

Jonna and I never played the what-if game, wondering what possibilities might have existed with Auburn if we had won fifteen games, or even ten, at Iowa State. I never considered giving

Auburn a call to express an interest in the opening. I remember thinking, *Wow, it's going to be crazy down there. I wonder what they're going to do.* I never checked to see who Auburn was talking to, and I didn't keep up with any of the speculation about the coaches who were considered top prospects. I kept busy recruiting for Iowa State, and that was that.

When Jamie informed me that Auburn had called, I asked if he had talked directly to Jay. Jamie said no, he had received a voice mail and planned to call Jay back the next morning.

I told Jamie that Jay probably just wanted to get some contacts from me for other potential candidates or to ask for some other type of help. But Jamie was convinced that Jay wanted to talk to me about interviewing for the head coach job. Jamie promised to get back with me as soon as he spoke to Jay.

Proper protocol for coach searches, to use this case as an example, would be for Jay to call Jamie and ask permission to speak with me about any interest I might have in the Auburn opening. Regrettably, that protocol isn't always followed, but Jay is a man of integrity, and he wanted Jamie's permission before he contacted me about interviewing with Auburn.

From the moment I hung up with Jamie until Jay's call on Saturday morning, my mind was swirling, trying to make sense of what I'd heard. Was it really possible that Jay was considering me for the job? *There's no way,* I thought.

As I anticipated the call from Jay, I considered what I knew of him from my time at Auburn. Jay is an Auburn guy through and through. With the exception of his last three years of high school, which he spent in Florida, he had lived near Auburn during most of his growing-up years. He returned to Auburn for college, walked onto the football team, earned a scholarship—not an easy task for a walk-on—and wound up lettering twice as an offensive lineman. He blocked for Bo Jackson, one of the greatest college running backs of all time, and started on the 1983 team that won a conference championship and finished with a number three ranking in the nation. By making it from walk-on to starter on a championship team, he proved early on that he wasn't afraid to attempt big things despite long odds.

He coached football at Auburn for a while, then took a job as an assistant athletic director and eventually worked his way up through the athletic department. For most of my time as defensive coordinator at Auburn, Jay was in a fund-raising department. He was promoted to athletic director right before Christmas 2004, just a month before I was hired at Texas. Although I never worked closely with Jay, his youngest daughter, Jayne, and my twin daughters were close friends. That meant we knew each other well enough for me to have a rather frank conversation with him the first time we talked about the coaching position at Auburn.

After a little small talk about our families, Jay got right to his purpose. "We've got a job opening," he said. "Would you be interested?"

"Jay, first of all, of course I'd be interested," I answered. "I know Auburn, and I can get the job done. There's no question in my mind. But I've got to ask: am I really in serious consideration for this? Iowa State has been great to me, and I am extremely happy."

I didn't want Jay to interview me as a favor to someone. I needed assurance that he was seriously interested in me. Otherwise there would be no reason for me to take this a step further.

"If we weren't serious about this," he said, "we wouldn't be having this conversation right now."

It finally sank in that Jay was considering me a candidate.

But how would he ever justify this possibility to everyone else at the school? With its winning tradition and consistently high expectations, Auburn could never flirt with the idea of hiring a 5–19 coach.

Jay didn't seem as concerned as I did; he wanted me to interview. I reminded him that the people at Iowa State had treated my family and me really well, I was starting to recruit solid players, and Jamie Pollard's decision to extend my contract assured me that I was secure in Ames. If any news leaked about my showing interest in another job, that would cause nothing but problems back in Iowa. It just wasn't worth the risk to interview for a job that was a long shot at best.

Jay responded by saying he was under a time crunch and he'd like to visit with me "real soon."

BACK TO DALLAS

As it happened, I was going to be in the Dallas area the following week to make recruiting visits and to undergo back surgery. Our trainer at Iowa State, Mark Coberley, had watched me suffer through back pain since I had arrived at the school. I wasn't able to stand up through complete practices, and I had to get injections of the painkiller Toradol just to be able to stand on the sideline for three to four hours during games. The pain was excruciating at times.

The week leading up to our final game of the 2008 season, Mark told me he couldn't watch me put myself through that pain any longer. He demanded that I get my back taken care of right after the season ended, and he set me up with a top-notch surgeon in Dallas. Of course, I tied the visit to the surgeon into a recruiting trip. I guess you could say that was my way of following Mark's orders while also justifying the trip with a football purpose.

I told Jay that Jonna and I could meet him there a couple of days after my surgery. Since we were already scheduled to be in Dallas for recruiting and medical reasons, I hoped no one would find out about my pending interview. I told Jay I'd be hobbling, I wouldn't have time to fully prepare, and I had no idea how coherent I would be during the interview, but he said that was fine. He knew a lot about me already, and he was aware of my history with Auburn.

With those concerns addressed, I took care of the proper protocol on my end. I wanted only two people at Iowa State to know about my interview with Auburn: Jamie and President Geoffroy. For one thing, I was convinced I wasn't going to get the job, so no one else needed to know. For another, I didn't want to toy with the emotions of the Iowa State fans. We had such a loyal following, and we felt there was a lot at stake from their perspective. They didn't deserve to have to face the ups and downs of media reports about whether their coach would leave. Jonna and I kept the interview so confidential that we didn't even tell our friends and family, our kids included.

In the late morning on Tuesday, December 9, I had surgery to trim a partially ruptured disc and cut away scar tissue. The next morning I left the hospital, and Jonna and I drove back to our hotel. I was not in good shape. My back hurt, and sleeping in a hospital bed the night before hadn't helped any. I was on pain medication, I moved with a slow shuffle, and I wasn't looking forward to sleeping on what I assumed would be another uncomfortable bed. I wanted to be back home in my own bed.

I was concerned about a news leak. My stress level was at its max.

I called Jay that evening. "Jay, I'm really nervous about this getting out. If I'm not one of the top guys, I don't even want to do this interview."

If I was only a top ten or even a top five candidate, I was out. In my mind, I had to be one of the top three candidates, because the more I thought about it, the more strongly I felt that the risk of my interest leaking to the media wasn't worth it. It was my dream job all right, but I had to know I was a serious candidate.

Jay didn't hesitate. "I can assure you that you're one of a couple we will consider," he said.

A ROUGH DAY FOR AN INTERVIEW

I felt awful Thursday morning, the day of the interview. My back was throbbing, I was still having trouble getting around, and my mind was foggy from the medication. Between the physical pain, the lack of time I'd had to prepare for the interview, and my concern about what would happen if people in Iowa found out, I had barely slept the night before. I tried to make a few notes for the interview in the hotel room, but I didn't even jot down enough to fill a page.

As Jonna drove me to the hotel where I'd be interviewing, I couldn't stop thinking about the people back at Iowa State. I had pledged to help turn the program around, and we were doing that. But now I was facing the possibility, as remote as it still appeared, that I might have to go back to Ames to tell all those people I was leaving. I don't know what it's like to cheat on a spouse, but on the ride over, I imagined the feeling had to be similar to what I was experiencing at that moment. I felt awful, and it wasn't just my back.

But at the same time, there was a little part of me that was ecstatic. Auburn was the place I wanted to be more than any other school in the country. I could see a move to Auburn as the last one I would make as a coach. It had become a destination job for me, the last stop for the rest of my career—however long that winds up being. The closer we got to the hotel, the more conflicted I felt inside.

My interview was scheduled for around lunchtime, and I had been told the search committee was meeting with another candidate before me. When Jonna pulled up to the hotel, I texted Jay to let him know I had arrived. He texted me back that the first interview was still going and he would contact me when they were ready. Jonna drove to a convenience store and we picked up some sodas and snacks. Then, to kill time, we drove around.

And around.

And around.

Perhaps because of the way I felt, Jonna and I didn't talk much. Or maybe I should say I don't remember us talking much. It could be that we talked a lot and I was so out of it that I don't remember. But one thing I do remember us talking about was the great situation we had at Iowa State. Not many 5–19 coaches receive such a vote of confidence. So as we waited for the interview, I had a nothing-to-lose mentality. We would have loved the opportunity to return to Auburn, but if it didn't happen, we had a good thing going at Iowa State.

Obviously, the only downside would be if news of my interview leaked. That was the one thing that made me uneasy. Otherwise, there was no stress to carry about the situation.

Well, except for the part about not feeling prepared for the interview. But there was nothing I could do about that at this point.

Finally, around 1 p.m., I received word that the previous

interview had finished. It had lasted much longer than I'd anticipated. That struck me as a good sign for that candidate . . . and
a bad one for me.

Jonna dropped me off, and I hobbled toward the hotel
entrance. I can't recall ever having to put so much effort into
taking short steps. I was in intense pain, and this wasn't exactly
the way I had pictured going into the biggest interview of my life.

On top of that, I was walking in empty handed. I am an
extremely detail-oriented person, and I put together thorough
presentations for job interviews—a half-inch binder with my
thirty-day plan, my ninety-day plan, and my one-year plan; my
calendars; my schedules; and my presentation. Today I just had
my bad back, my coaching history, and whatever gumption I
could muster. I took a breath and stepped inside the small meeting room.

I was relieved to see Jay and the other members of the search
committee, all of whom I knew from when I was at Auburn. It
gave me a boost of confidence that I already had some history
with them. I wasn't sure exactly how many candidates were being
interviewed, but I knew I had to be the least-prepared from a
presentation standpoint. Still, I was able to give the committee
members a good overview of the plan I'd implement if I were
chosen as Auburn's next coach, and I was confident in what I
was describing to them.

After all, I had just presented this plan two years earlier when
I had interviewed with Iowa State, and I had been working to put
the plan into place since then. I didn't need any PowerPoint slides
or presentation pieces because I had memorized my plan—in fact, I
had been living it. I described my intentions from pure experience.

While I wasn't able to give a blow-'em-away presentation,

looking back now I believe it was to my benefit that I could walk the committee members through my plan without laying it in front of them. Where I assume the other candidates had their papers and notebooks, I was able to tell off the top of my head and from the bottom of my heart what I would do at Auburn. Even with the pain and the medication, I knew what I wanted to do well enough that I could deliver it clearly and on point. No notes needed.

I didn't have anything to prove to these guys—they already knew me. They knew I stand for the right things in life, that I coach and live with integrity and complete honesty. They knew that I was an Auburn man at the core, a man of allegiance and conviction. They knew how familiar I was with the school, how well I understood the culture, how important it was to me to uphold Auburn's high standards—to do things the Auburn way. As for me, I knew what it would take to win at Auburn, and I knew we could do it.

But I was also 5–19.

I wasn't surprised that *the* question came up within the first fifteen minutes. Tim Jackson, an associate athletic director, asked, "If we hire you as the head coach, Gene, how in the world are we going to explain 5–19 to the public?"

It was a tough question, but I was ready.

"Please don't take this as being egotistical," I answered, "but let me ask you this question: if this was two years ago, how hard would this decision be?"

I paused.

I knew—all of us in that room knew—that publicly it would be difficult to defend hiring me. Maybe even impossible.

Tommy Tuberville, who had had one undefeated season at

Auburn and had led the Tigers to their first Southeastern Conference championship in fifteen years, was leaving after a five-win season. You don't need a math degree to see that his record in his last season outranked my five wins in two seasons.

I think everyone there knew that if I had been introduced as Auburn's head coach directly from being assistant head coach/co–defensive coordinator at Texas, it would have been an easier sell to the fans, alumni, and media. I would have been embraced as the Auburn man returning home to lead the program back to glory. But as it stood, I was going to have to dig myself out of a hole—a nineteen-loss hole.

I continued my answer. "My two years at Iowa State may keep you from hiring me for this job today," I said, "but the reality is I will be ten times the head coach for Auburn today than if you had hired me two years ago."

I could tell from the committee members' nods that my answer made perfect sense to them.

As the interview was wrapping up, I asked Jay about his time-table on making a decision.

"I don't know, Gene," he said with a shrug. "It could be twenty-four hours; it could be two days, seven days, ten days. I don't know what I'm gonna do."

That was not what I wanted to hear. I didn't like the uncertainty I detected in his voice, and I didn't relish the possibility that this ordeal could drag on for days and perhaps more than a week. We couldn't keep my interview a secret for that long.

EARLY PICKUP CALL

The first sign for Jonna that things hadn't gone well was when I called her to pick me up at the end of the interview. She had planned on reading at a library for three hours—maybe even four. I called Jonna to come pick me up only ninety minutes after the interview began.

"Remember the Iowa State job?" I asked her as soon as I'd shakily taken my seat in the car. "You know how I told you right after the interview I was confident I'd get the job?"

"Yeah," she said.

"This one—I ain't getting it."

"Why do you say that?"

"Trust me," I said. "I ain't getting it."

We both felt deflated and filled with a certain measure of regret. Here we'd agreed to this interview for a position I didn't really think I had a shot at, aware that more harm than good could come of it if people back home found out. The fact that my interview had been much shorter than the previous interviewee's, not to mention Jay's reluctance to commit to a firm timetable on making a decision, made me sure this risk would be all for nothing.

Jonna and I went out to dinner that night, but it certainly didn't have a celebratory feel to it. Jonna was just about in tears when the waiter came to the table and asked if he could take our order. All the stress and anxiety over the situation had become too overwhelming for her, so we decided to skip dinner and go back to the hotel to talk things through further. Later that night, after discussing it with Jonna, I decided to officially withdraw my name from the list of potential candidates. It just wasn't worth it. There was no way I was getting this job anyway, and I was feeling increasingly wary about having news of my interview somehow leak out.

The next morning, Friday, I woke up and checked my phone.

It was burning up with messages. Just as we'd feared, word had leaked about my interview. I still have no clue how, but it did. Meeting with Auburn had backfired on us completely. It had put the administration at Iowa State in a difficult spot.

I called Jay at Auburn and got his voice mail. I hated leaving this in a message, but I felt like I had to get it taken care of as soon as possible while we were preparing for a two-hour flight home. I didn't know if I'd be greeted by a media ambush when I returned to Iowa or what. "I'm getting ready to get on a plane and fly back to Des Moines," I said. "Listen, I really appreciate everything. I'm sure you've got great candidates for the job, and you're doing a great job there, and I know you guys will have a great coach. I'm just gonna bow out of this."

As soon as I left that message for Jay, I called Iowa State. I talked to Steve Malchow, the associate athletic director, since Jamie was out of pocket for a few hours. I told Steve I had called Auburn to withdraw my name from consideration. I added that I was about to board a plane to fly home and that when I was back in Ames, we could all sit down and prepare a statement addressing my interview for the job.

We'd meet the firestorm head-on. I felt a sense of loyalty to Iowa State and the administration, and I was ready for this entire ordeal to be over.

It sure seemed like a good plan.

We made it through the Des Moines airport and to our car without seeing any media. As Jonna drove, I checked my phone messages. There were two missed calls from Jay and a short message from him: "You have to call me when you land."

I called him and started talking before he could get a word in. "Hey, look, Jay, I'm sorry about that message. I hated to do it that way. I appreciate so much your thinking about me, but I'm gonna stay here at Iowa State and continue to build what I started."

There was a moment of silence as Jonna pulled into a McDonald's parking lot.

"Chiz," Jay broke the silence, "I want you to be the next head football coach at Auburn."

"I'm sorry; what did you say?"

"I want you to be the next head football coach at Auburn."

By this point, Jonna could hear what Jay was saying.

She got out of the car, desperate for a breath of fresh air. Both of us had been completely blindsided.

"Whoa, Jay," I said into the phone. "Man, whoa." I paused. So many things were suddenly sprinting through my head. "You have just blown my mind. Look, I'm excited, but I need to call you back. Let me talk to Jonna and then give you a call."

The awkward silence from Jay's end told me he was surprised that I even had to talk to Jonna before accepting the job. Jay's offer had totally floored me. I knew I could do the job, but until that moment, it had never seemed possible I would get the chance. I was blown away that Jay would make such a gutsy decision, knowing what he'd be up against as soon as the announcement was made. It was difficult for me to process at that moment. But make no mistake, I was humbled by Auburn's decision. And I knew this had to be a God appointment because this whole thing just didn't make sense otherwise. I knew God had to be behind opening this door—there was no other way it would have been opened.

I hung up, and Jonna got back in the car. We just looked at each other.

I smiled and shook my head before finally coming up with something to say. "Are you stinking kidding me?"

Both of us were silent for probably four or five minutes as Jonna drove north up Interstate 35 toward Ames. Neither of us really had words for what was happening, but there were points along the trip when we'd look at each other and just smile. My mind would flash over the debacle we had just come through— the surgery, the short time to prepare, the short interview, and of course, my 5–19 record. There was clearly something supernatural going on here—something that just didn't make sense in human terms.

After we began to get over our shock, I told Jonna that we needed to pray about the offer. I joke now that I told Jonna, "You pray, and I'll pack." But seriously, we prayed all the way back to Ames.

By the time we reached home, we knew that accepting this offer was the right thing for us to do. We also realized that the only way to describe these events was as part of God's plan. On the surface it seemed that my head coaching résumé had done nothing to earn the Auburn job offer. This was all God.

Jonna had latched on to Psalm 33:9-12 after we considered the question of whether we would be okay with losing for a period of time at Iowa State if we were doing what we believed God had called us to do there. When the Auburn job was offered to me, and as I sensed that it was a God thing and a God thing only, that passage also became central to my life. It reads:

When [the LORD] spoke, the world began!
It appeared at his command.

The LORD frustrates the plans of the nations
*   and thwarts all their schemes.*
But the LORD's plans stand firm forever;
*   his intentions can never be shaken.*
What joy for the nation whose God is the LORD,
*   whose people he has chosen as his inheritance.*

What that passage says to me is that God's plan is God's plan, and when God says he will do something, it doesn't matter what anyone else says or thinks. To personalize it, there are no circumstances in our lives that can prevent God from doing exactly as he pleases—even circumstances that would cause the outside world to look on and declare, "There's no way," "It can't happen," or "There's no hope." He has his own plan and his own timing, and both are perfect.

My being offered the Auburn job with a 5–19 record wasn't going to make sense to outsiders. From a football point of view, it didn't even make sense to me. It defied all odds. I couldn't explain it any other way than to say it was a God thing. If you've ever been through a 5–19 season in your life and God has created an opportunity for you that you didn't expect or consider possible, you understand exactly what I mean. And if you're going through one of those 5–19 stretches now, remain obedient to God. Live out the purpose he has given you. He has a plan that stands firm forever. His intentions can never be shaken. His plan will open up for you even when there are a million reasons why it can't happen.

Our God *is* bigger than 5–19.

5

....

A BITTER ENDING

PROFESSIONALLY, ACCEPTING THE AUBURN JOB was a no-brainer. Personally, leaving Iowa State was agonizing.

We don't operate with a "Got something better; see ya later" mentality. I felt like I was letting down the school, the fans, and especially the team. I had been responsible for recruiting the new players, and some of them had come all the way from Florida and Texas. These guys had put their faith in me when they made the decision to join us in Iowa. They had parents back home who had trusted me with their kids.

When I came to Iowa State, I wasn't looking at it as a short-term plan or a stepping-stone. Jonna and I didn't necessarily see it as our last coaching stop or the spot where we'd ultimately end up as a family, but we also didn't consider Iowa State a place we'd stay only long enough to show what I could do as a head coach and then move on to another school.

Coaches hope to avoid moving when their kids are older, especially, say, right before their senior year in high school. Senior year should be a special time in their lives, not a transition year. Our twin daughters, our oldest kids, were nine when we moved to Iowa, so we had plenty of time before they reached their late high school years.

My vision was to recruit and build a team from the ground up. I signed on with Iowa State to develop a winning program, not a couple of winning teams. We had barely had a chance to see what these talented young players could bring to the team and what kind of core we could build, and now here I was considering leaving after two years—well before that dream could be realized.

Not only that, but my family had become a part of the Ames community. Jonna had gotten involved with organizations such as the Boys & Girls Club and an agency that worked with children in foster care as they aged out of the system. She also sought out various projects we could help with by lending our name, especially projects that involved kids. Since our children played just about every sport available to them, we became active in rec sports programs, and there were various school activities we were part of too. In a short amount of time, we had developed a number of deep friendships.

We knew it would be hard to leave Iowa State. As it turned out, it became more problematic than it should have been.

OUT OF CONTROL IN A HURRY

My transition from Iowa State to Auburn was no doubt the most difficult forty-eight hours of my career. I still tell Jonna I'm convinced those two days took a year, maybe two, off my life.

From the moment I heard from Jamie Pollard that Auburn wanted to talk to me about its open job, things started happening rapid-fire.

On Thursday I interviewed with Auburn in Dallas. On Friday news of my interview leaked and I decided to withdraw my name from consideration; then I was unexpectedly offered the job. And that wasn't even the wild part of the ride. The real chaos was still to come.

After prayer, soul-searching, and talking it over with Jonna, I called Jay Jacobs to inform him that I wanted the job. I arranged to meet with Jay and the Auburn president, Jay Gogue, between our two schools, in Memphis, Tennessee, the next day. If all went well for both sides, I would sign the initial term of agreement. I called Jamie to inform him that Auburn had offered me the job and that I intended to go to Memphis to meet with Jay and President Gogue. We were still holding our cards close at this point—we knew that until I put pen to paper, nothing was official.

On Saturday Jonna and I flew to Memphis to solidify the deal. I could hardly believe it, but this was really happening. I had landed my dream job. The first phone call I made from Memphis was to Jamie to let him know that Auburn had officially offered me the job and I had accepted.

As difficult as it was for me to leave Iowa State, the struggle was a personal one, not a legal one. Coaches leave schools before their contracts expire all the time. Our contracts contain buyout clauses and all kinds of legal provisions to allow for that, and Auburn officials would check with Iowa State to find out what was required to buy out my contract.

Auburn arranged for Jonna and me to spend Saturday night in Memphis. We would fly to Ames on Sunday morning, pack our necessities, then fly to Auburn later that afternoon. On Monday morning I'd be at a press conference announcing my hiring.

After meeting with Jay and President Gogue in our hotel suite and signing the initial agreement, Jonna and I fell into bed, exhausted, thinking we'd finally have a few hours of peace and quiet. That wasn't to be. You know that expression about the ink having barely dried? That was true in this case. We turned on ESPN, and not even twenty minutes after I had signed the contract, there was my name, scrolling along the bottom of the screen with the news that I had been hired at Auburn.

Other than Jamie, we had not told anyone yet, and here it was being broadcast across the country on ESPN. Our family, our friends, the players back at Iowa State, and all the school's fans were seeing on TV that I was leaving. We were stunned that this was being reported so quickly. How had ESPN found out? Neither of us had a good answer.

Our cell phones started exploding with calls and texts from what seemed like every family member and friend who knew our cell numbers. They wanted to know if what they were hearing was true.

It was. I was the new head coach of the Auburn Tigers. And now everyone was finding out.

As I sat there watching ESPN, my thoughts flew immediately to my players. I hated the thought of their learning on television I was leaving while I was in a hotel room three states away.

Our return to Ames was a frosty one, to say the least. Jamie and President Geoffroy were not happy I was leaving. I wish the announcement hadn't panned out the way it did, but I'd done everything I could to keep the school informed every step of the process. I never wanted to leave on a negative note.

Jamie and I had had a great relationship up to that point. I still admire many of his leadership skills, especially the strength he showed in standing up to our opponents when we created the life skills assistant position. I appreciated the way he supported me during our losing streak and his confidence in me despite our 5–19 record. Jamie is a quality athletic director, and I respect him for what he has done at Iowa State. But I wish he had handled my departure differently. It could have, and should have, gone so much better for all involved.

On Saturday, shortly after the news went public, Jamie issued a statement saying, "I'm disappointed for our Iowa State fans and student-athletes that he has chosen to leave our program after only two seasons. I understand that [Auburn] is a dream job for him, but the timing and the way it played out has been hurtful and disappointing. Although this is a significant setback, we will get through the challenge because the Iowa State University athletics program is far greater than one person."

I agreed with him on that last point.

Looking back now, I realize how much pressure this situation put on Jamie as an athletic director. I also know that the timing is never good for a coach to leave a school for a better opportunity. Regardless of when I had left, it would have been difficult for the folks at Iowa State.

When I had talked to Jamie, I told him that before I left, I wanted to meet with him and President Geoffroy, then the players. Jamie said he and the president did not need to meet with me. I was disappointed that Jamie was not in favor of having a face-to-face meeting to talk about the situation. We had talked about everything during our two years together. If we could have sat down and discussed the matter and ironed out any miscommunications, I believe we could have prevented the negative tone surrounding my departure.

I might not have gotten the closure I was looking for with the Iowa State administration, but when it came to my team, I knew there was no way around it: I had some good-byes to say. No matter what, I was going to meet with the players.

SAYING FAREWELL

First would be a wrenching meeting that Sunday morning with my coaching staff. We had all been together for two years working to rebuild this program, and they had been selling our vision and long-range plan to players and recruits, too.

I was literally sick to my stomach before the meeting. Some of my best friends, including guys I'd known for up to twenty years, were waiting for me in our meeting room. One had been in my wedding and served as a pallbearer at my dad's funeral. I was scared by the thought that some of those true, down-to-the-bone friendships might be ruined by my leaving.

When a coach leaves, those who stay behind know that the new coach will bring in a new staff of people he is comfortable with. With my departure, suddenly their jobs were no longer secure. And with the perception battle I would be facing at Auburn, I knew I wouldn't be able to take most of them to Alabama with me. I would be a tough-enough sell on my own; there was no way I could convince the folks at Auburn to take on an entire staff with a losing record.

When I walked into the room, all the coaches were quiet. I could see the uncertainty on their faces as I took my usual spot in front of them. I couldn't help but realize that it wasn't only the lives of fifteen coaches that were being thrown into uncertainty but also the stability of fifteen families.

I told the coaches how events had unfolded—that I had not sought out the Auburn job or put in a phone call to say I was interested. I apologized that I had not been able to share with them that I was interviewing for the job. For one thing, I explained to them, I had considered my chances of getting the job a long shot. For another, I like to conduct my business in private. Essentially I wanted to apologize that they hadn't heard from me personally when I'd accepted the job. I didn't want to do things behind their backs, but this had been an altogether different set of circumstances.

I then informed the coaches that I would meet with each one individually to give him an idea of whether I would be considering him for a position at Auburn. I knew that people would be hurt in this process, but I tried to convey that none of it was purposeful on my part.

Finally I requested that each of them be at the team meeting I was about to hold. I wanted to have us all together in front of the team one more time. I asked for feedback on what they had heard about the players' reactions, and they told me the players were angry and upset.

The coaches handled the meeting with class, and afterward they congratulated me on the Auburn job. They were professionals, and they knew how our business works. Unfortunately, I did wind up damaging some friendships by the time I had filled my staff at Auburn. Most of those relationships have since been restored, but there are still some residual hard feelings. What helps me today is knowing that every one of those coaches has found good employment at either the college or the professional level. Still, I continue to work on healing some of those relationships that were damaged.

As tough as the good-byes were, I was proud of the shape we were leaving the football program in. We'd brought in good players, and all our guys had learned how to compete in a tough conference during our two years there. The tone of the team had improved, and the players had dug deeper in terms of their discipline and commitment. And perhaps best of all, there was also the lasting spiritual legacy to be grateful for.

That morning, before I met with the coaches, I had called Ken Sheppard, the strength and conditioning coach, and asked him to call a team meeting. I wanted Ken to meet with the players before I did so he could let them know I would be explaining the situation to them. With the negative spin they had been hearing about my leaving, I wanted to give them a chance to calm down before I talked with them.

Ken met with the players in the locker room, then had them move to our team meeting room. With my back still in great pain, I gingerly walked up the flight of stairs toward the meeting room. I felt like I was walking the green mile. As I climbed the stairs, I thought about my promises to the players' parents that I would be at Iowa State with their sons, and now here I was leaving. I distinctly remember thinking about parents who walk out on their children and wondering what could cause them to do such a thing. I mean, these weren't even my children, and I had been with them only a year or two, but I still couldn't get out of my mind the sense of a parent abandoning his children.

It gnawed at me to realize that in that room there were a hundred or so young men I was leaving, most of whom I would never see again.

One of the expectations I have at team meetings is for players to sit up straight with their feet on the floor and to maintain eye contact with the speaker. But when I walked into the meeting room that day, the players' body language spoke volumes. Many of them were slumped in their seats or leaning to one side. Some were looking at the floor or off to the side—anywhere except my eyes. Even an amateur at reading body language could tell the players were upset. I'm sure that because of what they had been hearing, they felt like I had deceived them and was walking out on them.

I was brief and to the point, and my message was simple. I told the players that I loved them and that for two years I had done everything I could to help them grow as athletes and as men. I told them I was sorry we hadn't won more games. Then I gave them my vote of confidence that they could be a great team. "I believe Iowa State has a great future because of you—because of each player in this room," I told them. "You are men of character, and you won't skip a beat without me." I said I would be watching them and I looked forward to seeing them win.

In bringing the meeting to a close, I apologized for leaving and explained why I was going to Auburn. "This move makes the most sense for me and my family," I said. "We are from the South, and the Auburn job is a good fit." I looked from one player to the next. "Although I am looking forward to going to Auburn, it hurts me deeply to leave you. But this move is something I need to do for my family." I reminded my players that I loved them and said they could call me if they ever needed me for anything.

That was it. The meeting lasted probably five minutes.

Under better circumstances, I would have allowed the players to ask questions. But because of the way events had taken place,

I couldn't see any good coming out of an open-forum Q&A session. More than half the players in that room were guys our staff had recruited to Iowa State. I had visited many of them in their homes during the recruiting periods. I had sat across the living room from their parents, looked them in the eyes, and told them I would take care of their sons while they were at our school. Their sons had come to Ames so we could all work together to bring winning football to Iowa State. Now here I was walking out of the meeting room while the players remained behind for another meeting. There wasn't an opportunity to talk with any of them one-on-one, to thank them individually for what they had done with us at the school. It certainly wasn't the good-bye I would have planned, but I was glad I was able to speak from my heart and tell them exactly how I felt.

I wish things would have unfolded differently. I wish someone from the administration would have said to the players, "Here's what happened. This is part of the territory in college football—if you have a good coach, other schools often want to hire your coach. Now we'll go out and get another good one. We're going to miss Coach Chizik, but we're going to wish him the best because this is the best decision for him and his family. We appreciate Coach Chizik's two years here, and we are committed to going out and bringing in another good coach."

That didn't happen.

No player said a word as I walked out of the meeting room. It dawned on me that in a strange way, their body posture and evident anger made a positive statement about our relationship. Their nonverbals indicated that they believed in the direction the program was headed. They were mad and, in a sense, communicating that they'd rather have us stay.

I made my way down the stairs, handed the keys for my school-owned car to associate athletic director David Harris, gathered the few belongings in my office, and walked out of the building.

There was ice on the ground and it was snowing as I carefully short-stepped my way to a car driven by a graduate assistant coach I had asked to take me home. I got in and closed the passenger door, and neither of us said a word. As he pulled out of the parking lot, I looked back at the athletic facilities. *Wow,* I thought. *This is it. I'm probably never coming back here.*

As Jonna and I have reflected on our time at Ames, we've thought about how God challenged us to rethink our definition of success. In light of that perspective, I figure that if bringing a chaplain into the football program is the one thing I'm remembered for at Iowa State, I'm good with that. When it comes down to it, knowing that a player grew spiritually during his time at Iowa State means more to me than any stats or records.

TAKING OFF

When I arrived home from the school, it was time for Jonna and me to tell our kids we were moving. The night before, while we were in Memphis, they had stayed with Mark Coberley, the Iowa State trainer, and his wife, Denise, who had children our kids' ages. We hadn't told even our kids or Mark and Denise why we were going to Memphis. "Can you please keep our kids overnight?" we had asked. "We can't go into detail about why, but we'd like you to keep them for us." Mark and Denise never asked any questions. But on Saturday evening their TV was turned to ESPN when the ticker began scrolling that I had accepted the Auburn job. They quickly turned off the TV before our kids could see the news, and they kept it off the rest of the night.

So when we got home, the kids still did not know. All three of them burst out crying when Jonna and I told them the news. We tried to point out the positives, such as the fact that we were going back to Auburn, where the twins especially had made good friends, and how we viewed Auburn as a place where we could finally settle down. Still, the news was upsetting for them. The day had started with two extremely painful meetings for me at Iowa State, and now we had moved on to another difficult scene at home, with Kennedy, Landry, and Cally shedding tears.

On top of all that, we faced hard feelings from the community, too. I understood how sudden it must have been for fans to hear the news that I was leaving. But a coach can't just take out a full-page ad in the newspaper and announce that he is going to interview for another job. I had communicated my plans to the people from Iowa State who needed to know. For the rest of the community, though, we knew the news came as a shock.

Still, we weren't prepared for how quickly things turned hostile. To us the environment was beginning to feel poisonous. Jamie's statement questioning the timing of my decision and expressing his disappointment over his perception of how the process had played out added to an already-negative atmosphere.

As we packed for our trip to Auburn, friends were calling us and sending us messages informing us how bitter the comments were becoming on local radio shows and online forums. It was unlike anything we had ever been through. All our other coaching moves had been fairly positive. But as the day progressed, the environment in Ames seemed to grow increasingly tense. We even wound up losing friends because we were leaving. That hurt because those friends had been influenced by the negative tone coming from the administration. You obviously don't expect a parade out of town when you leave one school for another, but this was even more difficult than we'd anticipated.

Ideally we would have flown as a family for the introduction at Auburn, and then Jonna and the kids would have returned to Ames to stay in school at least until spring break. With all the negative reactions, however, we felt more comfortable having our family together in Auburn.

As adults who have experienced our share of the public spotlight, Jonna and I are used to criticism and have learned to block it out. But it was different for our kids. We didn't want people's criticisms to reach them. Coaches' kids catch enough grief at school after their dad's team loses a game—we didn't want them to be subjected to more negative comments the next week about my leaving. So we decided to hastily pack up what we could and move the entire family to Auburn. Jonna was packing so fast that when she opened the suitcases later, she discovered that she had brought at least three single shoes . . . without their matches! I failed to pack all my suits but one.

We'd had our home in Ames built to our specifications, and it was the home we'd always wanted. Now we weren't even able to properly close up our dream house and put it on the market. We'd have to come back later to finish packing and get the house ready to sell, but for now all we could think about was getting on that plane for Auburn as soon as we could.

In Jamie's first news conference after I left Iowa State, on the Monday I was introduced in Auburn, he called my character into question, saying my actions during the interview process did not match the values he had observed in our two years together.

I have a personal policy of not defending myself in the media, and I adhere to it strictly. From my perspective, it is not productive or necessary to stand up for my honor through a public forum. I've decided that the only people whose opinions I have the energy to worry about are the ones in my small, trusted circle. I will defend my players publicly, but in terms of my own reputation, I choose not to get involved in back-and-forths in the media even if, as in this case, that means I am portrayed as something I'm not. People who truly know me for who I am know the truth, and the truth always wins out.

It was a difficult time for Jonna and me, but since then we've been able to gain some closure and move on. Jamie and Jonna have had a couple of conversations since that time, and he sent us a lengthy, handwritten letter, mailed from his home to ours. They have talked through what happened concerning our departure, and Jonna has been able to find peace about it. I have not had a conversation with him since I left Iowa State, but I don't hold any grudges. I know this is just part of the business I'm in, and I'm the type of person who moves on quickly. After two good years of working for Jamie, I was disappointed about how the final forty-eight hours panned out.

Two fantastic years at Iowa State came to an end with two really horrible days. There was even a parting shot for us at the airport. As our family boarded Auburn's jet, with the big *AU* on the tail, we saw two men standing outside the fence. They were holding signs that read "Roll Tide"—the slogan of Auburn's fiercest rival, Alabama.

I'll never forget how freezing cold it was that day and what a relief it was when the plane's wheels lifted off the runway. As the plane ascended, lifting us from the storm below, I looked down and took a deep breath. *Finally, some peace,* I thought.

Even as I left the Ames community, I couldn't shake one continuous thought: *When I get to Auburn, it's not going to get much easier.*

6

·········

WELCOME HOME

THE PLANE'S WHEELS were barely off the ground before it was time to gear up for our new life at Auburn.

Auburn's public relations and sports information personnel were on the flight with us, and we spent the two hours preparing for the Monday morning press conference—my first public appearance since accepting the job.

We envisioned every possible scenario at the press conference and tried to anticipate any topic that might come up. The PR folks asked me round after round of questions, and I answered with sample responses. We prepped for the first twenty-four hours in Auburn, starting with the moment we landed at the airport, and went through each event with a fine-tooth comb. Being Mr. Preparation, I was into every detail.

It was evening when we landed, and I was shocked to see that there were hundreds of people at the Auburn airport. At that point I wasn't sure if they were there to hang me or hug me!

As we approached the crowd, I could see that people were holding up signs. I couldn't read the messages, and I honestly didn't know whether they would be positive or negative. Would these fans be prepared to welcome a coach with a ten-game losing streak? When we got close enough to read the first sign, I breathed a sigh of relief. It said, "Welcome back to Auburn, Coach Chizik."

This might be a friendly crowd after all, I thought. *Besides, I don't see a police escort around here.* For all I knew, the people in the crowd might have been coerced or paid to be there, but at that point I didn't care. It was a comfort to see happy people, even if they were only faking it.

As I looked out at the mass of people, all I saw and heard were cheering fans, plus a handful of players I had recruited to Auburn but never coached because I moved to Texas. I appreciated those guys coming out to welcome me.

Auburn's mayor was there, and during a short presentation, he handed me a key to the city. The cheerleaders and the school mascot were there as well, adding to the celebratory feel of the evening. I addressed the fans for two or three minutes, then went into the crowd and shook a lot of hands. The job was new, but the place wasn't. I enjoyed walking through the crush of fans and meeting up with a number of people I had become friends with my first time around at Auburn. It had been five years since I had seen most of them, and I kept noticing how much their kids had grown in that span. Even Kennedy and Landry, who were eleven at the time, felt at home when they saw friends at the airport they hadn't seen since we moved to Texas, including Jay Jacobs's three daughters. To our surprise, it felt like we'd been greeted with not just a "Welcome" but a "Welcome home."

THE DREADED MOMENT

The first stop after the airport was the one I dreaded most. Item number one on my agenda was to meet with the members of the coaching staff who had lost their head coach. This meeting had been one of the dark clouds looming over me since accepting the job.

The coaches were gathered at the athletic office waiting for me. I knew most of the guys from my previous time at Auburn. And after sitting at that same table for countless meetings myself, I even knew where each of them would be sitting. As we drove from the airport to the office, I pictured it all in my mind, going around the table face by face.

Sure enough, when I walked in, to the best of my recollection, each member of the coaching staff was in his same seat. Except this time my spot wasn't just to the right of Tommy Tuberville's chair. This time Tommy's old seat—the one at the head of the table—was reserved for me. It was a strange feeling the first time I took that chair. Nothing was different about the chair itself, but everything was different for me. I was now the head coach. And I had come to that table to deliver bad news.

I looked at the faces around the table, then got right to the point. "Guys, I know this is hard for you. Really, really hard. And it's not easy for me, either. A lot of you are my friends, and I've kept in touch with you since I left. So this is one of the toughest things I've ever had to do. We all know that in this business there are some hard decisions that have to be made. And I hope that none of you take these decisions personally because it doesn't mean you're not a good coach. It doesn't mean you're not a good recruiter. It doesn't mean you're not a good person. But the bottom line is, I have to come in here and do what I think is best to get Auburn where it needs to be. And you know there's a good chance that no one in here is going to be able to stay with me. So my advice to you is to go out and look for a job, and I will help you in any way I can. If I feel like you're a good fit for what we're trying to do, I will call you back. But right now, you have to assume that you don't have a job."

You have to assume that you don't have a job. I knew those words had to be difficult for the coaches to hear. But I did not want to give any of them false hope. As much as I didn't want to deliver those words, it would have been far worse for me to lead anybody on regarding his chances of remaining at Auburn, then let him go when he thought he had a shot to stay. To me, the best thing to do for those coaches was to go the opposite way—tell them what they didn't want to hear. Then if I decided any of them should stay, I'd call them in and talk about offering them a job.

I wound up keeping only three of the twenty-five or so members of the previous staff (graduate assistants included). There were two I knew I wanted to keep from the outset: Kevin Yoxall, the strength and conditioning coach, and Chette Williams, our chaplain. It has been humorously pointed out to me that the first two people I kept worked with strength and faith. The third person who stayed on was Phillip Lolley, who would fill the spot of cornerbacks coach for us.

Taking away the jobs and security of almost a complete staff is one of the ugliest parts of the coaching business—especially when friends are involved. As hard as it was to let so many friends go, that call was all mine. The Auburn administration had left it up to me to determine what I wanted to do in assembling a staff. I could keep the people I thought would be the best fit and not bring back the ones who weren't. The school's administrators indicated to me that they felt the need for a new beginning, but they gave me complete freedom to effect that change as I saw fit. I thought the best way to do that was a complete overhaul of the program, and that included the coaching staff. For the sake of the players especially, I felt we needed to start from scratch.

Tommy Tuberville had been at Auburn ten seasons. But this was the beginning of a new era, and our styles were completely different. Some of the staff members had been with Tommy all ten years, and they were accustomed to doing things Tommy's way. I was creating a fresh start, making a complete change—in everything from program philosophy to recruiting. I know that when an assistant coach has been working within one system for as many years as most of these coaches had, the transition to an entirely new system can be difficult and requires a certain adjustment period. To make the new beginning Auburn needed, I had to have coaches who were 100 percent behind my way of doing things from the very start. It was necessary for every chair in that meeting room to be filled by someone with complete allegiance to my vision.

Whether the coaches saw this coming or not, they were true professionals during the meeting. I know it wasn't easy for them to hear they needed to look for work elsewhere, but I left the room that evening appreciating the way they had handled the news.

Unfortunately, I wound up losing friends over the decisions I made. Some of the coaches in the meeting understood that this was what amounted to a business decision. Others, however, wound up taking my decision personally. What hurt was knowing that Gene Chizik, the former Auburn defensive coordinator, was the same person as Gene Chizik, the new Auburn head coach. I hadn't changed, but my title had. And with that, perceptions of me appeared to have changed too.

I struggled with knowing that some of the coaches who had lost their jobs were thinking, *Boy, look at him. Now he's got the head coaching job, and he has changed.* I knew that wasn't true, and frankly, I didn't think it was fair. We coaches know the profession. We know that the hiring and firing in our business is messed up sometimes. But I was hired by Auburn to do what I thought was best for the school and the football program, and that's what I did. That meant firing the staff and then hiring the people who would match our program's vision most effectively.

Many factors go into hiring and firing decisions like these. It's easy to think that friendship should be the determining factor, but it doesn't work that way. If a head coach bases personnel selections on people he's friends with, the team's record will suffer and the entire coaching staff will soon be looking for work. Ultimately, a head coach has to hire and fire with his players in mind.

Some of the coaches who lost their jobs at Auburn didn't talk to me for a while. A few still haven't. After I became head coach, we played a game with one of the former coaches on the opposing sideline. We had been good friends for almost two decades before I returned to Auburn. Before the game, I sought out the coach to shake his hand. It was an awkward moment at best. He barely looked me in the eyes, and although he did shake my hand, he did so grudgingly. His reaction shocked me. At that point I decided, *You know, I'm going to continue to try to reach out to my former friends, but I need to be prepared for the worst.*

Jonna and I have agonized over the lost friendships from both Iowa State and Auburn. I hate the thought that coaches who lost their jobs probably think of me as the bad guy whenever they hear my name or see me. But since Jonna and I believe so strongly that friendships are worth reconciling, we are committed to trying to reconnect with some of those people who were hurt during the transition.

Just like when I left Iowa State, my arrival at Auburn complicated the lives of more people than the coaches. There were about forty families at two schools almost a thousand miles apart who in one day saw their lives suddenly thrown into a state of uncertainty. All because I moved from one job to another.

IT'S NOT ABOUT YOU

Immediately after the coaches' meeting, I faced my second appointment: meeting with my new players. On the way downstairs to the meeting room, I thought about my final time with the guys from Iowa State and how upset they were about their coach's leaving.

The Auburn players were in the same situation, although at least in this case there had been almost two weeks between when they had learned that Coach Tuberville was leaving and the announcement that I was replacing him. In the meeting with the Iowa State players, I had to deal with the fact that the players were getting a negative spin on my resignation from every avenue, every source. At Auburn, I was up against a similar dilemma, but in this case, the players were getting a negative spin on my *hiring*!

Media and Auburn supporters alike were asking how the school could hire a 5–19 coach.

I could tell my record had preceded me when I entered the meeting to see several players wearing skeptical looks on their faces. I did, though, find comfort in knowing that a small number of players I had recruited when I was defensive coordinator were still here. I knew I had at least a little bit of credibility in the room.

Again, I was short and to the point.

The first topic I touched on was trust, but probably with a different slant than the players expected.

"I don't trust you, and you don't trust me," I said bluntly. That certainly got their attention. "But nine months from now, we'll get there. I promise, we'll get there. There'll be a lot of ups and downs, and it won't be easy. But we'll get there."

I explained that our team would not take the path of least resistance. We were going to build our program the right way. More than that, we would do everything the Auburn way. I emphasized to the players the importance of having allegiance to Auburn and all the great people and athletes who had worn the Tigers uniform before them.

"That's what we're going to be about here," I continued. "We're going to be about Auburn. It's not about you—it's about everybody else but you."

I recited for the players the first two lines of the Auburn Creed, written in the 1940s by George Petrie, a professor and coach of Auburn's first football team in 1892. The creed's words have become a set of beliefs and principles shared by the school's students, faculty, and alumni. It describes the Auburn way and has become not only an inspiration for Auburn but also a symbol of the school. I still knew the words from my first time at Auburn:

I believe that this is a practical world and that I can count only on what I earn. Therefore, I believe in work, hard work.

A sign in the Auburn weight room reads, "Work, hard work." I figured most of the players didn't know where the words on that sign came from, and I wanted them to have that background.

If we could get every person in that meeting room to live out those words, we would develop trust with each other. I told the players there was no doubt in my heart that we would achieve that goal.

I don't know what the players thought about my speech, but I liked it.

I also liked that it was my last speech of the day. The press conference was scheduled for the next morning, but for today at least, my taxing meetings had come to an end. Thank goodness.

Throughout the day I kept praying, *God, please get me through this day. Just get me through this day.* I knew I was going to need his peace and comfort if I was going to make it. I needed to hear God say, *It will be okay. It's all good.* As tough as the press conference would be, it was nothing compared to looking into the eyes of the two coaching staffs and the two sets of players I had met with that day.

HIS STRENGTH, NOT MINE

I hadn't eaten all day, but I wasn't hungry. My mind was still swirling with the events of the past few hours. I was exhausted, but I had a feeling I wouldn't be able to sleep well that night.

By the time Jonna, the kids, and I checked in to our hotel that evening, we were completely drained—physically, mentally, and emotionally. I had signed my letter of agreement with Auburn only the day before, and now here we were in Alabama, a world away from Iowa. We'd just begun to process the idea that we'd all be moving to Auburn, but none of us had expected that it would happen this fast.

When we walked into our suite, we were greeted with a pleasant surprise: the Auburn athletic department had bombarded us with Auburn gear. Hats, sweats, T-shirts, shorts—just about anything Auburn-related you could imagine—were spread all over the place. The kids were thrilled and couldn't stop running around the room to check out their new clothes. *Wow,* I thought. *This is one of the rare moments today when anybody's been really happy.*

What should have been one of the happiest days of our lives, and a time to bask in the realization of a goal we had been dreaming of for so many years, had instead become a painful, stressful stretch for all of us—a time I never want to relive. If all went as I hoped here, there would be no more leaving Jonna behind with the kids to pick up the pieces while I went to the next job. No more moving the family to new schools and new churches. No more being an absent father for several months while the kids finished up school in another state. No more having to make new friends while wondering if we'd have to start all over in another couple of years. No more walking into a roomful of coaches and saying, "I'm not going to keep you. You should start looking for another job."

As is often the case in life, the dream-come-true parts were intermingled with the tough realities. We were eleven days from

Christmas, and everyone was stressed—my wife, my kids, and certainly me. I knew we were making the right move, and I knew this opportunity was what I had been working toward. Most significant, we knew getting this job was a God thing. But still, the getting there was really painful.

God, I prayed, *in my weakness, show your strength.* Based on how I felt that night, there were plenty of opportunities for him to do just that.

MEET THE PRESS

As expected, I didn't sleep much Sunday night. *One more day,* I told myself Monday morning. I would meet with the media, and then I would get straight to work on recruiting and hiring a new staff.

Ah, football. Finally.

But first, the media.

With my 5–19 record, we knew it probably wouldn't be a favorable Q&A session. But my goal going in wasn't to win the press conference. I just wanted to be me.

Jay made an opening statement, introducing me as the right man for the job. That was the theme I had emphasized to the search committee in Dallas, and it was something I planned to impress on the media that day.

"I am excited and proud to stand before you today and announce Gene Chizik as our next head football coach here at Auburn University," Jay began. "We know we brought the best man back to Auburn who is fit for the job. To Gene and Jonna, Kennedy, Landry, and Cally Chizik, welcome back to Auburn. You're right where you belong."

I couldn't have agreed more. We were right where we belonged.

After a few more short remarks from Jay, it was my turn for an opening statement. I began with Auburn fans' favorite two words: "War Eagle." After I thanked Jay and President Gogue, I expressed what a special day this was for me. Then I looked at Jay.

I'm sure there were moments while making his decision when Jay asked himself what he was doing or wondered if he had lost his mind. It took strength on his part to pick me out of all the candidates and then to follow through on his decision despite skepticism from around the country. I don't know of anyone other than Jay who would have hired me in the same situation. Okay, perhaps my wife would have. But from the beginning, I wanted to prove to Jay that he had indeed hired the right person for the job.

"Jay," I said to him, "I want to tell you that you hired the right guy. There is no doubt in my mind. This is a dream. When you go into coaching and you travel around for twenty-three different years, you always want to know, 'Where is my final destination?' The coaching profession is kind of a transient world; you move here and you move there. But my beautiful wife, Jonna, and my family, we always have the conversation about where we are going to end up and where we want to be. As the years traveled on and certainly after we left Auburn, we always wanted to come back. This is a blessing for me, a very special day."

I'll admit that I got a little long-winded with my opening statement, going on for nearly ten minutes. But that first press conference was an opportunity for me to set the tone for the changes coming to the program. I talked about the vision President Gogue and Jay possessed for the university and the athletic program, as evidenced by the new basketball arena, the student union building, and student housing that had been added since I left for Texas. Auburn was definitely moving forward. I promised to recruit tirelessly and reestablish relationships with the state's high school coaches. I also emphasized to former Auburn players that our football program's doors were wide open to them and that we aimed to build a program that would make them proud to tell people they were Auburn Tigers.

I pointed out Carlos Rogers, a cornerback for the Washington Redskins, who had asked permission from the Redskins to fly in for my introduction. Antarrious Williams and Bret Eddins also were there. All three had been defensive players on our undefeated 2004 team. All three were also walking examples of what we wanted Auburn players to be: good athletes on the field, quality people off the field, and successful contributors in their chosen professions. These players had believed in me when I was at Auburn, and it meant a lot to me to have them there to show their support. Mike Wright, my former pastor, drove in from Birmingham to be with us at the press conference too, and he prayed with Jonna and me beforehand. It was good to feel we had some built-in community at Auburn from the very beginning.

One of my final remarks before opening the floor to questions was "Our goal is to win championships and to produce some great men out of this university." I ended by reiterating to Jay that he had hired the right guy, and then it was the reporters' turn to ask questions.

Of course, there were questions about my two years at Iowa State (although no one actually used the phrase "5 and 19").

First I was asked about Iowa State going 2–10 for the just-finished season.

"I'm going to back up a little bit on that question and give you a little bit of insight into the whole situation. Two years ago when

I took that job, I was ready to be a head coach. To be honest with you, I'd really done everything I could do as an assistant. I went back-to-back undefeated seasons, I'd been a part of a national championship, and I was really blessed to win the Broyles Award my last year here at Auburn. I was ready. When you decide to venture out when you're ready to be a head coach, some jobs are more challenging than others. So it's not like I walked into Iowa State and I knew it wasn't a challenge—it was a challenge. However, I had a blueprint in place for what we were going to do, and I knew it was going to take time. I put that blueprint into effect, and I never deviated off it one bit. We played eleven true freshmen this past year, and that was part of the plan. So that being said, those two years that I gained as a head coach were invaluable. I wouldn't change it or do it over again any different. If it was exactly the way it was ordained, those are the same steps I would take over again today."

Then I was asked whether I left the Iowa State program in better shape than it was when I arrived.

"I don't think there's any question. The hardest thing about me moving on from that job was having to face that football team yesterday because there were relationships there. I recruited some really good players there, and it's hard to say good-bye. That was hard. But unequivocally, two years removed from the day I got there, it was a better place."

Finally I was asked how much of a challenge it would be to get Auburn fans on board with me in light of their negative reaction to my record at Iowa State.

"I think that answer is really easy. You have to win. There is going to be skepticism no matter who you hire . . . whether your record is 6–6 or 7–5 or 4–8. There are going to be people who agree with it, and there are going to be people who don't agree with it. I'm smart enough to know that. At the end of the day, right now, what I do know is that this was the right hire for Auburn. What I do know, at the end of the day, is that this . . . is a dream job for me because I understand this place. I understand these people, I understand how to recruit it, and I understand the importance and passion and energy of this place. The people who are going to be negative, I can't control. That's out there for everybody to mull over themselves. But at the end of the day, when you win, I think all of that goes away."

One of the big issues we had anticipated and prepared for did indeed come. It was a question about our archrival, Alabama, and its head coach, Nick Saban.

Nick had led Louisiana State—another SEC school—to a national championship in 2003. He later coached the Miami Dolphins and then returned to the college level to coach at Alabama in 2007. He turned Alabama's program around and in 2008 led the Crimson Tide to an undefeated regular season, including a 36–0 victory against Auburn. Alabama ended up losing in the SEC Championship Game and then in the Sugar Bowl, but the damage had been done. Nick had temporarily moved Alabama ahead of Auburn on the field and in recruiting. That was a big problem for the Auburn family.

The rivalry between Auburn and Alabama is one of the biggest in the nation, and the coach of either team will inevitably have to field questions about his cross-state opponent. It doesn't matter if Auburn is playing LSU, Arkansas, Ole Miss, or any other school in the coming week, there's always a chance an Alabama question will get thrown into the mix. So we were pretty sure the Nick Saban/Alabama topic would pop up at some point.

I was not about to get into any kind of Gene Chizik versus Nick Saban conversations. It's Auburn versus Alabama, and trust me, that's big enough. No need to create any rivalry beyond that. So I avoided talking about Nick altogether in my answer when the reporter asked about coaching in the SEC and against Nick and Alabama.

Since the reporter mentioned the SEC in his question, I took advantage of that opening to talk about the challenge of competing against SEC schools as a whole, then included how Alabama was part of that challenge.

"I think you said it really well the first time—it's the whole league," I began. "Obviously any in-state rivalry is always big, wherever you go. I've been a part of some really great ones, obviously this one as well. But it's not just Alabama; it's the whole league. I'm looking forward to it. I love recruiting. I can't wait. We're going to get out there and throw it around. All of that's the exciting part of the job. That's the part you gotta love. But it's everybody in this league. Because this league, from top to bottom—everybody knows that it's the best out there. It'll be a challenge for the whole league, and Alabama is always in that challenge."

That answer wasn't going to stop the Gene versus Nick questions, and frankly nothing will, but at least early on I was demonstrating that I was not going to be drawn into those one-upmanship conversations.

Despite some challenging questions, I felt we had prepared well and I'd been able to answer every question with confidence. There's no scoreboard for these media sessions, so I can't say whether it was a win or not. But I was pleased with the tone we set in my first public appearance as Auburn's head coach.

More than that, though, I was glad to have all the meetings behind me. Probably fifteen minutes after answering the final question, I was on the recruiting trail and off to visit a high school. I was ready to get down to the football part of being a football coach.

7

BEGINNING THE TURNAROUND

I RETURNED to an Auburn program that was different from the one I had left several years earlier. In my three seasons as defensive coordinator, we had compiled a 30–9 record. My final season, in 2004, we had a 13–0 record and won the Southeastern Conference Championship.

After defeating Tennessee in the SEC Championship Game, we were ranked third in the Bowl Championship Series rankings. The top two teams in the rankings at the end of the regular season play each other to determine the national champion, and USC and Oklahoma were ranked first and second, respectively.

We were one of five undefeated teams that year, but because we were third in the BCS rankings, we didn't have an opportunity to play for the national title. We knew in our hearts that we deserved a chance to play for the national championship and at least show what we were capable of. The BCS system is controversial, and each year there are outcries for a major overhaul. That season the system didn't work in our favor, but there was nothing we could do about it. We had beaten the teams on our schedule, and that was all that was under our control.

Instead of playing for the national title, we played in the Sugar Bowl in New Orleans, where we beat ninth-ranked Virginia Tech 16–13. When USC beat Oklahoma in the Orange Bowl—that season's designated BCS Championship Game—we jumped to second in the two major college football rankings: the Associated Press Poll (determined by news media) and the *USA Today* Coaches' Poll (determined by college football coaches).

Despite finishing undefeated for only the fifth time in Auburn history, we had to settle for being number two and believing that we could have won the school's second national championship. USC later had to vacate its championship because of NCAA sanctions. That decision has been appealed, but even if the appeal is denied, Auburn would not be named the national champion for that season. We would have preferred to have won the championship on the Orange Bowl field anyway, not in some NCAA meeting room.

That was the way I left Auburn—on a streak of wins. That's not the way things were when I came back. During the seasons I was with the Texas Longhorns, Auburn had 9–3 and 10–2 records. In my first year at Iowa State, Auburn finished 9–4. In 2008, Auburn was number ten in the Associated Press preseason rankings and number eleven in the coaches' rankings. That turned out to be a season of unmet expectations.

The Tigers won their first three games and were 4–1 after five games but struggled from that point on, losing six of their final seven games. The last game was a 36–0 shutout at Alabama—Auburn's worst loss to Alabama in forty-six years. Auburn fans didn't take the loss well, as you can imagine. That put Auburn's final record at 5–7 and ended a streak of eight consecutive seasons of playing in a postseason bowl game.

I knew I had some ground to recover when I took over as head coach. Immediately after reporting to work at Auburn, in addition to recruiting high school players and beginning to assemble a new coaching staff, I started meeting one-on-one with the players. I needed to take the team's pulse and get a feel for what was going on at the players' level.

My conversations with the athletes revealed that I was taking over a team that was emotionally drained. The struggles of the previous losing season had taken a toll on the players. There were obvious divisions throughout the team, and the splits were along multiple lines—between offensive and defensive players, between younger players and upperclassmen. I sensed that there were cliques on the team, and there even appeared to be division along racial lines.

Players on the team told me, "Well, I don't really know this guy because I never hang out with him." Or "I live over here in my apartment, and he's over there in the dorm. I don't know much about him." Or "Those guys have this issue or that issue they need to deal with." Every direction I turned, I could see glaring disconnects within the team.

Juniors told me they wanted to give up and quit football their senior year. Younger players said they were ready to call it a career too or transfer to play at another school. One of the top players told me that he no longer loved Auburn football. It wasn't that he didn't love football, he clarified; it was that he didn't love

Auburn football. With the respect and appreciation for Auburn's football tradition I had developed during my first tenure here, it pained me deeply to hear a player—a star player, especially—say those words. I love Auburn football, and I want every player who comes through the program to feel the same.

As the player meetings continued, it became increasingly clear that we had a divided, shattered team. I don't know how the team became that way, but the on-field product was obviously being adversely affected. The players' responses to one question cemented to me just how much the team needed an attitude overhaul.

I'd tell the players, "Don't give me the company line on this. Shoot straight with me. If it's the third, maybe fourth, quarter and we're down by two touchdowns, can we win the game?" The predominant answer was along the lines of "It would be real difficult." Some just flat out said no. That's a sure sign of a team that is not confident.

But at least now I knew the major problems we had to address.

TEAM BUILDING

One of the first remedies I put in place to wipe out divisions was to hold team events. These connections off the field, I believed, would eventually build trust among the players on the field.

We look for every opportunity to hold team events, and we try to be as creative as possible with what we do together. We've had movie nights and bowling nights. We've hosted freshman skit nights, where all the new players—not just freshmen—divide into groups and perform skits for the rest of the team. We've even held an impromptu Halloween costume contest.

One time when we were in the thick of those intense two-a-days during the summer, we stopped practice early and told the players to change their clothes and be ready to leave in ten minutes or else return to finish practice. They sprinted to get out of their football gear and were thrilled to learn we were headed to a water park. A number of them hadn't been to a water park before, and it was funny to see how many guys said they wouldn't dare get on any of the waterslides . . . until the other players did and some good-natured peer pressure began.

Once, we took the players out to a farm, fed them a meal, and held a fishing competition.

On the surface those just sound like fun outings. They took us out of a football setting and away from the common denominator that had brought us all together: Auburn football. At a deeper level, though, those trips were really about breaking down walls.

Take our fishing competition, for example. Football players are competitive, so even fishing carried an element of challenge for our guys. They couldn't wait to see who could catch the most or the biggest fish. Most important, nobody wanted to fail.

What happened was that in order not to fail, players who didn't know how to fish had to rely on tips and advice from their more experienced teammates. Some of the guys would go to another group to ask how to bait a hook. Or how to cast. Or how to reel in a fish and take it off the hook.

Forgive me for picking on the linemen here, but there's something undeniably funny about watching a big, mean lineman beaming like a little kid after reeling in a fish that isn't even big enough to fillet for dinner. And then there were the tough guys who live by a "no fear" motto on the field but were now scared to grasp a wriggling fish to take it off the hook.

We shared a bunch of laughs when we went fishing, and our

stories lasted well into the season. But in the process, we were accomplishing our larger purpose: putting our players in positions where they had to trust their teammates.

In addition to the team-building outings, we implemented some changes closer to the field too. For starters, we switched up all the players' locker assignments. Puzzled expressions filled the locker room the first time the guys walked in and discovered that the names on all the lockers had been rearranged. The players had been used to lockering next to their buddies. They'd go to their section with the same five buddies around them every day, all season and all off-season. But we switched things up so that no one had a locker next to a teammate he knew well.

Players searched for their lockers and found an offensive lineman next to a defensive back. Or a wide receiver next to a defensive end. Because we divide up by positions so often in football—in meetings, film sessions, practices, etc.—it's possible for an offensive player to go through his entire college career and barely know a teammate on the defense. I had a vision for something better. In my view, building relationships is one of the longest-lasting benefits of playing college football, and I had decided to do my part to "force" relationship building across the different segments of the team.

This shifting around of players' lockers wasn't a onetime occurrence either. We rearrange locker assignments every year. We make it convenient for players to get to know different teammates each season.

We also switched up all the meeting rooms. The offensive linemen, for example, had used the same meeting room for ten seasons. Not anymore—we moved them to a different room. Same with the defensive linemen. No part of the team met in the same room as before. If it was the old way of doing things, I didn't want us to do it that way anymore. In some instances, that was for no other reason than simply to shake things up—to make a bold statement to the players that we were entering a new and different era.

DELIVERING THE MESSAGE

I knew we needed to instill Auburn values in our players, and one of my strategies for doing that was to hold constant team meetings. I knew that in previous seasons there had been few full-team meetings. There's nothing wrong with that; I just have a different style. I believed that getting everyone together in one room—especially in the early days—would be beneficial in educating the players on the way our program would be going about business.

There was another advantage to having full-team meetings instead of smaller ones led by coordinators or position coaches: they allowed me to deliver my message personally—not only *what* I wanted said, but also *how* I wanted it said. Because of all the divisions we were trying to erase, we needed one voice in front of the entire team hammering home the same message over and over again.

We used PowerPoint presentations, videos, talks, props—whatever method we thought would help our players grasp our message. With a group of a hundred or more pupils—our players—we used every method of learning imaginable over the course of a season. We tried as many different approaches as we could so that every player could learn through the style that was most effective for him. It's easy, and certainly less time consuming, for a coach or a leader to teach using the method by which he teaches best. But if the goal is for the audience to learn what is being taught, you have to teach in the way each member learns best.

Football wasn't our only subject in team meetings. Wise decision making is a big theme of mine. I want the players to consider how many choices they make each day, how their choices today affect what they do tomorrow, and how many people other than themselves their choices potentially impact.

Case in point: a player could choose to skip classes, which could lead to his failing a course and that would lead to his being ineligible to play. Then the entire team would suffer from having one player fewer on the depth chart. We even take it a step further. If a player becomes ineligible, his family suffers, too, because his parents have to answer questions at work and from friends about why their son isn't playing. Younger brothers and sisters face the same questions at school. We try to make a player think about all the people who are affected when he doesn't do what he is supposed to do.

I know it's not easy for a nineteen- or twenty-year-old to drag himself out of bed to attend an 8 a.m. biology class. But the truth is, the entire team needs him to choose to get up and go to class instead of sleeping in. He's not just attending that class for himself, but also for his one hundred or so teammates. If he thinks about those teammates wanting to win a championship instead of how tired he is when that alarm goes off in the morning, he's going to be more motivated to kick off those covers and get his tail to class.

It works the same way for just about every decision players make on a daily basis. So I use our team meetings to drive home points that move the players toward being more others-centered instead of self-centered. I teach a team concept for everything we do—not only on the football field, but in everyday life.

From the beginning, I have encouraged the coordinators and position coaches to make their meeting rooms their own. I want them to put their favorite sayings and quotes on the walls. This is a chance for the coaches to emphasize their philosophies and what they believe in. When the players walk into their respective meeting rooms each day, they face these big, bold reminders of what is important to their coaches. I want everything we put on the walls to be informational, educational, and inspirational.

One of the first things we did before my initial season was repaint all the walls, and we hung pictures of NFL players from Auburn: Carlos Rogers. Karlos Dansby. Jason Campbell. Ronnie Brown. Cadillac Williams. Bo Jackson. Kevin Greene. James Brooks. Auburn has been blessed with a number of high NFL draft picks, and our players know who they were. They want to become NFL players like those guys who have gone before them, so the pictures immediately inspire respect and awe.

Those pictures remind our players of what they can become if they work hard and accomplish great things together as a team. Many of our guys dream of having their pictures hanging on those walls one day, and we are showing them that we want to help them accomplish that goal. That can't happen, of course, unless we trust each other.

I had told the players in that first meeting that I didn't trust them and they didn't trust me, but we were starting to change that. Little by little, we were creating an environment of confidence in and reliance on each other.

SHARING OUR STORIES

One thing that struck me early on at Auburn was that the players didn't spend much time in our athletic offices. They didn't seem to want to be in our building unless they had to be. I told the coaches during a meeting, "Look, here's the deal with these kids. If they're not up and down these hallways wanting to be in our offices, if they're not up here to see us—not when there's football going on, not when they have to be here for a meeting, not when you have them here to chew them out—if they're not wanting to hang out here, then we're doing something wrong."

We turned the bottom floor of our athletic offices into a players' hangout. We brought in Ping-Pong tables, pool tables, air hockey, video games, couches—anything that would make them want to be there.

All of a sudden, they started spending more time around us. After they'd attended their classes, eaten lunch, and completed their homework, instead of going back to their dorm rooms or apartments, they would come hang out at our offices.

Our coaches would wander through the downstairs area and spot a kicker playing pool with an offensive lineman and a receiver challenging a linebacker to a game of air hockey. They weren't necessarily becoming best friends, but they were spending time together and getting to know each other. Players also got to know the entire coaching staff, not just their position coaches. The lines of separation—by football position, age, religion, and race—were being erased.

A turning point in our relationship building came after we had started two-a-days in late summer heading into our first season. The changes we had made to break down the divisions among players were working. The locker room switches and the new lounge area were having the desired effect. But I realized that we coaches didn't know the players' stories. We were making progress, but we still had room to get to know each other at a deeper level.

I wanted to open things up among our players and coaches. So when I'd sense that perhaps the practice routine was becoming monotonous for the players or they really didn't want to sit through another session of breaking down and scrutinizing film of our practice, I'd tell the coaches, "All right. Tonight we're not going to watch film. Tonight you're going to have two or three of your kids tell their stories."

I believed it would benefit us as a coaching staff to learn more about our players. It's said that everyone has a story, but too often we don't know the stories of the people closest to us. I wanted to be intentional about setting aside time for us to sit down and listen and really get to know each other.

Knowing where kids have come from or what they're going through at the moment gives us a better idea as to why a particular player is having a bad day. When we learn how a player was brought up or what struggles he's facing, we can help him in his life outside of football too.

It's amazing what we learn when players share their stories. You might think that these big, tough guys would stand up and not really want to say much about their personal lives. But I'm telling you, once most of them start talking, you can't stop them. It's as though they have just been waiting for someone to ask what they have to say.

At various schools I've coached at throughout my career where we've created opportunities for players to share their stories, we've heard accounts that are mind blowing. I remember one player telling us about how he had contemplated killing his mother's boyfriend because the boyfriend had beaten her up almost daily. Another player shared the story of witnessing a relative get accidentally shot and killed on a hunting trip. One discovered the body of a parent who had committed suicide. There have been stories of players who were abandoned and left to raise their siblings, players with parents in prison, and players with family members and friends who were tangled up in gang violence. You just never know what has taken place or is currently taking place in a player's life.

I've learned that players appreciate having a forum to share their struggles and successes away from football. Sometimes those guys get painted into the football corner to the exclusion of everything else, but they are young men—still kids, in many ways—who need guidance and support. They need people who will express an interest in the non-football part of their lives.

Those sharing times have been a great vehicle for getting to know our players better. They help us formulate a sense of who our team is. We've had situations where a player tells us that his mother is battling cancer, and then when that player has to leave early on a Friday to go home, a teammate or a coach steps up and says, "Hey, guys, we need to pray for him and his mom." When the player returns on Monday, his teammates and coaches squeeze his big, burly shoulder and ask, "How are you doing, man? How's your mother? We prayed for you. Is there anything you need?"

Gradually everyone on our team developed a good sense of what everyone else was dealing with, and they started taking a personal interest in each other's lives. We didn't create this type of environment to win football games. We did it because God placed within each of us the deep need for relationships. But I will tell you that based on what I've repeatedly observed in my two-plus decades of coaching, players and coaches will do far more on a practice field and a game field for people who care about them and are investing in them than they will for teammates and coaches they barely know.

I tell our coaches that we can't work our players more than we care about them. If the players know that we love them and that's the reason we work them so hard on the practice field and in the weight room, they will push themselves because they understand we have their best interests in mind.

This kind of environment creates a bond between players and a sense of allegiance to the teammates playing next to them on the field. The players are more willing to battle hard for a guy when they know his struggles, when they know what he's going through. The more they learn about a teammate, the more he becomes like a brother. Knowledge leads to trust, and trust leads to a team becoming a true family.

We have to expedite that bonding process at the college level because we don't have the luxury of time like a lot of high school programs do. On a high school team, there may be players who have been attending school together since their elementary days. They played in the same leagues as kids and came up through middle school together. A high school team can have a core of players who have known each other for eight, ten, maybe twelve years.

At the college level we have a short window of time to develop a cohesive bond. We are bringing in players who have never met each other. They're from different parts of the country; they're different races; they're from different socioeconomic backgrounds. They're thick and thin, big and little. They may have very little in common other than football. We have to bring them together quickly so that when our team is down by two touchdowns, they trust their teammates enough to know that they can come from behind and win that game.

The quarterback has to trust the receiver to make the catch. The cornerbacks and linebackers have to trust the safeties to provide help in pass coverages. The coaches have to trust the players to carry out their assignments on offense and defense. The players have to trust the coaches so that when the team is down by fourteen points in the second half, they believe the coaches can make the adjustments and put them in position to overcome that deficit and win. When circumstances don't look good for a victory, trust becomes the determining factor in whether you will win anyway.

Now let's carry over that sense of trust to when players are off the field. Let's say a player is close to making a really bad decision. A good teammate will step up and say, "I'm not gonna let you do that. I care about you too much to let you make that mistake. You're coming with me, and I'm gonna get you out of this place where you could make a poor choice."

Or maybe a guy is slacking off in his classes. I've seen our players step in and say, "I'm gonna come get you, and you're going to class with me." I've seen older teammates say, "I'm gonna go get my car, pick you up, and make sure you're in class."

I've also heard one player tell another, "Oh, you have a makeup workout at 5:30 in the morning? You know what, if you're late on this one, it's gonna be a rough two weeks for you. I won't let that happen. I'm gonna come and pick you up. I'll make sure you don't oversleep, and I'll drive you to the workout."

When you see those situations playing out within your program, you know you have a special group of guys capable of accomplishing great things together—on and off the field.

8

A SOLID FOUNDATION

I KNEW IN THE EARLY DAYS as Auburn's head coach that I would have to be patient in allowing the players to build up faith in our program. But I didn't wait at all to build up the presence of faith itself.

Faith is an integral part of our team. I can't count how many times someone has commended our team because they've seen our players praying before or after games. We don't hide the fact that our players are free to pray on the field. We're not embarrassed to be seen praying because we're not embarrassed about our faith. When you are a praying person, that's who you are and what you do, no matter where you are.

In contrast to Iowa State, where we had built the chaplain's position from scratch, Auburn already had an established spiritual environment. Chette Williams, the team chaplain, had been with the program since 1999, and I was excited to be reuniting with him. Keeping Chette as the team chaplain was one of the easiest decisions I've made in my career. I had big plans for him, and they were just as important to me as anything I wanted to do with the offense or the defense.

"We've got to ramp up the FCA presence on the team," I told Chette in my first days on the job. "I want you to eat lunch with players in the cafeteria. I want you to have as many one-on-one meetings with them as you can. I want them to feel like they can talk to you about what's going on in their lives. We need to identify the guys who are struggling or seem like they're lost in their personal lives. We need to help them get their lives straightened out and get their priorities in order. That will bring them back into the team atmosphere we're building here."

I also told Chette that I wanted our players to get to know each other at deeper levels and develop strong bonds. I wanted them to feel comfortable discussing issues together as they were going on. The absolute worst way to deal with issues is to have players form cliques and talk about other players. That only creates more problems. Those types of discussions are divisive, and our team had far too much division already.

"We've got to start talking about all the tough topics," I told Chette. "We need to dialogue about offense-defense issues. I want us to start talking about racial tensions and cliques—about all these groups that are dividing us. We've got to bring our players back together—white, black, Christian, non-Christian, linemen, defensive backs."

Before my relationship with God began deepening in 2002, I had separated football and faith. They were two important areas in my life, but I'd never brought the two together. Football was over here, faith was over there, and I kept each on its respective side of the line I had drawn between them. But once I began to bring the two together in my personal life, I was amazed at how well they complemented each other.

As I grew spiritually, I started feeling that I should go out on a limb more and share my faith with the players. That prompted me to decide that once a year at a players' devotional, I would take fifteen or twenty minutes to tell the players about my spiritual journey. Much like I wanted our coaches to know the players' stories, I wanted the players to know my spiritual story.

The players at the different places I had coached knew I was a Christian, and I had always striven to model for them what it looks like to live by a code of integrity. But I sensed that God wanted me to be bolder about sharing my message and more transparent in letting the players know why I try to live the right way: because first and foremost, I want to serve God.

After becoming aware of the opportunity I have to change lives for eternity, I stepped out further on that limb and became more open about saying, "Here's who I am spiritually. If you ever want to talk to me about it, if you ever want to know more about God, this is who I am and what I believe." In addition to having a football program that provides its players with spiritual resources to help them through the struggles college athletes face, I realized that I should offer myself as a spiritual resource as well. This wasn't a radical, overnight transformation for me; it was more of a gradual maturation process. I didn't wake up one morning as a preacher or an evangelist. But as I grew closer to God, I felt more compelled to share what he had done and was doing in my life.

I joined a weekly men's Bible study at Auburn, and I noticed a gradual impact. I remember one study we did on Ephesians 6 about putting on the whole armor of God. Those discussions about all the different pieces of spiritual armor available to us allowed me to feel a sense of protection from the stresses of my job.

I started having lunches with our pastors, Mike and Sue Wright. We'd talk about what was happening in our lives and how God desired to play an active role in those everyday events. Those talks gave me confidence to be more transparent in front of my players, especially when it came to my annual devotional talk.

With each step in my spiritual maturation, I began to notice more openings to share my faith with the players. It felt like God was creating natural openings for me to let my guys know how important my faith and my beliefs are to me.

It's important to point out that we've never forced Christianity on anyone in our program. We have players who choose not to take part in FCA and players who aren't Christians. We are not an FCA program that has a football team; we are a football team that has an FCA program. I am not the chaplain; I am the head coach. I was brought to Auburn to win football championships. I hire coaches, I recruit players, and I make decisions on who gets playing time. I don't ask who was at the last FCA meeting when I make those decisions. I play the guys who give the Auburn Tigers the best chance to win championships. I'm a football guy. But I'm no longer a football coach throughout the week and a Christian only on Sundays when I'm at church. Those two components of my life can no longer be separated.

I now choose to live out my faith in front of my coaching staff and my players. I unashamedly tell them about my relationship with God. I don't preach, but I do make it a point to impart in our program values and concepts that are also part of a Christian lifestyle: service, obedience, faithfulness, loyalty. And I give my full effort to lead by example in those areas.

Interestingly, I've realized over the years how similar the paths to success are in football and in faith. In order to have a successful team, I knew we'd need to do three things: establish trust, build discipline, and weed out selfishness. Those are the same essentials that define success on God's terms. As Christians, we must place our complete trust in God. We must have daily discipline in our spiritual lives, with prayer and Bible study as the most prominent examples. And we must remove our selfish motives and replace them with a mentality of service to others.

I've seen firsthand what an integral role those values play in both arenas, and that is one reason I am convinced that faith and football work well together. That's why we established an environment in our program in which coaches and players are encouraged to thrive spiritually.

Friday nights before games, we have optional prayer meetings at our team hotel, whether it's a home game or a road game. (For home games we bus the team to a hotel out of town to get them away from all the local hype for the next day's game.) Attendance at these meetings is strictly voluntary, and no coach is there taking roll.

Coaches do show up on occasion, but typically the Friday night prayer meetings are a time for players only. Friday nights have become a safe haven for the guys, and I've heard story after story of how players have used that time to spill their hearts out in front of their teammates. There's a freedom in those meetings to share what's going on in their lives and express their hurts and needs.

I'm often amazed by how many guys go to these gatherings. They take place at 9:00 or 9:30 the night before a game, after a long day of walk-throughs, meetings, and a team meal. It would be easy for a player to just head up to his hotel room to relax before the big game the next day. But instead, most of the players choose to be in that prayer meeting.

I believe that one reason these meetings are so well attended is because of the strong Christian leaders on our team. Other players look up to these leaders and see that they have their priorities in order. There is just something different about them—the way their lives match up with their talk, the level of peace that flows out of them, and even the way they treat other people. And if these leaders happen to be guys who carry their Bibles around or lead FCA groups and prayer meetings, that's all the better. It provides them with an opportunity to share the message of what success truly is and the role God plays in helping them achieve that success.

That's why I've broken down my previous barriers between football and faith. And that's why I can comfortably stand in front of my team and announce that there's an upcoming prayer meeting, then encourage anyone who is interested to attend. I pray that as I do that, the players see a head coach who is standing firm in his beliefs and is not ashamed of that.

KINDERGARTEN RULES

One of the first concepts I began instilling in our players is what I call my "kindergarten rules." These aren't a written set of rules, and we don't keep an updated list, but during my character talks, I emphasize these basic rules to live by.

I call them kindergarten rules because they are things we were all taught in kindergarten: Say, "Yes, sir," and "No, sir;" "Yes, ma'am," and "No, ma'am." Remove your hat when indoors. Push in your chair when you leave a desk or a table. Clean up your mess when you finish your meal in the cafeteria, then take your tray to the proper place. Offer a firm handshake when you meet someone, and look the person in the eyes. Treat people the way you want to be treated. And so on.

I think it was our second or third team meeting when I introduced the kindergarten rules, telling the players, "You all think you're too cool for this stuff, but we're not into cool at Auburn. This is the way we expect you to act."

One day I was sitting in the cafeteria and saw two players leaving their trays on the table after they'd finished eating. It was time for a kindergarten rules lesson.

I approached the players. "So who do you think should take your trays back up there for you? You want the cafeteria workers to come get your stuff?"

The two guys knew they were busted. "No, sir," they replied sheepishly, then cleaned up their messes and picked up their trays to return them.

My message to them was that they didn't deserve any special treatment and that they were no different from any other students on campus. Just because they were football players on a full athletic scholarship, that didn't mean they deserved to have someone else cleaning up after them. They needed someone to help them see the error in their thinking. I certainly don't mind being that guy.

Ideally, we wouldn't have to reeducate eighteen-, nineteen-, and twenty-year-olds on the simple principles of how to act properly in public, but these guys have led a sort of charmed existence during most of their young adulthood. They can come in with a look-at-me attitude.

Here's what happens. These players reach high school as

good athletes, and then they start being recruited by colleges. Recruiting has changed drastically during my coaching career, and now it's almost impossible for a high school athlete to escape the recruiting process without an overinflated sense of self. With the way technology puts so much information at our fingertips, recruits come in having read countless articles about themselves. They love hearing the press about themselves, being on television, and having coaches, media, and recruiting services calling them to talk about which school they're going to attend. They are unknowingly becoming trapped by the attention. With five-star recruits—the top-rated and most-coveted players—people all across the country are treating them like they're rock stars. Being immersed in an environment like that, they become accustomed to thinking that everything is about them. Then when they show up at college, they get a startling wake-up call.

After a coaching staff has signed its recruiting class, it now has twenty-five guys who have all spent the past several months being told how important they are. That's twenty-five guys who think it's all about them. That's a problem.

This mind-set also runs counter to what we teach in our program. Early in the season I tell the players, "It appears to me that the problem on this team is that you think people are here to serve you. You are not here to be served. As a matter of fact, you were placed on this earth not to be served but to serve. You're here to humble yourself and care for others. So we're going to get rid of that old way of thinking. We're going to remove that from your mind. That's not what we're here for, and this is not about you. This is about football, this is about team, this is about family, and this is about Auburn. Playing football at Auburn is not a right; it is a privilege.

"I know what you are thinking. But like it or not, things are going to change. Starting today. If that's a problem for you, there's an exit sign above that door right over there, and you're all welcome to pass under it. I've got no problem with that. But if you want to stay here, you're going to have to serve others, not sit around waiting to be served. If you want to stay here, you're gonna have to do things the Auburn way."

If we are going to build an allegiance to this place, the players first need to understand that everything is not about them. They need to understand that we play for Auburn. They need to understand that we play for a lot of people who put it on the line long before they got here. They need to understand that this place was made great way before they ever arrived, and if they leave tomorrow, the place will still be great. I bluntly tell the players, "You're not going to change Auburn. Auburn will not become you—you will become Auburn."

It takes a while for that message to begin to register with the players, but we continue to pound the "It's not about you" truth into their minds. I tell the players that I don't want them to develop an allegiance to Auburn *after* they leave; my desire is for them to develop an allegiance while they are still here. I don't want them to go through college and at some point after graduation think, *You know, Auburn was really great. I loved Auburn. Wow—I never thought I'd miss it this much!*

I want the players to begin to realize in the midst of it what a blessing and a privilege it is to play football at Auburn. I hope they take advantage of the moment while they are in it. They may not be at that point of understanding yet, but I know they'll get there if we are persistent in preaching that message.

We instituted freshman meetings my first year at Auburn, and we've kept them going. Our goal is to start molding their thought processes from the day they come on board at Auburn. We want them to consider why they are here and appreciate the privilege they have been given. We talk about serving rather than being served. We discuss the recruiting process and how the reality of our program is the opposite of what they've heard from most other schools that recruited them. We counsel the freshmen on adjusting to college life. We get to hear the struggles they go through, and players thrive knowing their coaches care about their lives.

Three of our coaches—Phillip Lolley, Curtis Luper, and Trooper Taylor—are at every freshman meeting. I attend as many as I can because I want to hear personally what the freshmen are experiencing. When I'm unable to attend, the coaches always bring me feedback on what took place. That's how important the discussions in these meetings are to me.

One of the most effective tools we've used in these freshman meetings is to have each player write a letter of appreciation to someone who has helped him reach this point in his life or perhaps has even changed his life. The letter must be handwritten, and the player must address the envelope himself. You might laugh at this, but we've actually had to instruct players on how to do this properly. Some have never addressed an envelope by hand before.

It doesn't matter whom they write to. It can be a mom, a dad, a coach, an aunt or an uncle, a grandmother, a mentor. But every freshman must write one letter.

We've been blown away by the impact those letters have had. We had some cases where a player wrote to his high school football coach and the coach was so proud of the letter that he read it to his whole football team. Then our player received forty letters from the kids on that football team.

I don't know how many times a parent has told me or one of our coaches, "You know what? I really appreciated that letter because I didn't know that's what my son thought of me. I didn't know that's how he really felt." Our players might have had these thoughts for a long time but never shared them with the person who needed to hear them.

It's the seemingly little things like a handwritten letter that have the potential to make a significant difference in someone's life.

A FATHER'S INFLUENCE

Many of these character-building concepts I pass on to my players are a direct result of the influence my father and mother had on me. No person has had a bigger impact on my life than my dad. He meant so much to me that I asked him to be the best man at my wedding.

Dad was a great man who was respected because he treated everyone fairly. He was a man's man—he was straightforward, and if he was committed to doing something, you could take that to the bank.

I confess I had a touch of show-off in me as a young athlete. I'll admit to even being a little cocky. I'd be shooting baskets with a look-at-me demeanor, and my dad would stop my shooting and say, "Son, don't tell me. Just show me." He said those words to me so many times that I can still hear him saying them in his no-nonsense tone. *"Don't tell me. Just show me."*

"If you show me you can do something," he'd continue, "I'll know it. Don't tell people how good you're gonna be. Don't tell people you're gonna get this done. If you just do it, then people will know it." He would repeatedly drive that point home to me—probably because I needed to hear it repeatedly.

My dad grew up around the time of the Depression and served in World War II, but as is common with men from his generation, Dad wasn't the most expressive person on earth. He would always tell me I had done a good job when I accomplished something, but he wouldn't say much beyond that. I wanted more than anything in the world to please him, but at times it was difficult to know for sure whether I had.

It wasn't until after I married Jonna that Dad and I would say that we loved each other. Dad wasn't the touchy-feely, sentimental type who would go around saying, "I love you" all the time. But I always knew he did. Without a doubt. He might not have said it, but he always showed me he loved me by how he treated and raised me and by the time he spent with me.

"Don't tell me. Just show me."

I used to love the times we'd throw a ball around in our yard. I never heard him bragging about me to others, but I could see the look of pride on his face. The people around my dad could tell he cared about me too. Dad had a way of clearly communicating genuine love and affirmation without using words.

I was Dad's only boy. I have three older sisters, Patricia, Marianne, and Rita. He loved us all, but I felt a special bond as his only son. I inherited my name (Eugene) and my sports DNA from Dad. He played football on scholarship at Rollins College outside Orlando and became a junior high and high school football coach in Florida before moving into school administration.

When Dad took the job as principal of Largo High School, he moved our family to nearby Clearwater. I didn't understand at the time why he made that decision. Clearwater and Largo high schools were big-time rivals back then. It was about as huge as a high school rivalry could get.

I became captain of the Clearwater football team while Dad was principal at our rival school. Not until I was an adult did I finally learn why Dad had moved us: he'd had the foresight to make sure everything I achieved would be viewed as my own accomplishments, not as a result of his being my principal. It's easy now to wish he would have told me then why he'd made that decision, but I don't think at that age I would have fully understood anyway. And that was just my dad's style: to quietly do the right thing.

Dad also had an indelible work ethic. He worked his tail off. He didn't make much money in education, and with four kids to feed and clothe, he also drove a taxicab at night.

My mom, Rita, was a hard worker too. She started her shift as a nurse at 11 p.m. She would get off work at 7 a.m., come straight home, get us kids ready, take us to school, and go home and sleep for a few hours before picking us up from school, helping us with our homework, cooking dinner for the family, then getting ready to go to work again. Dad would always tell us, "There's no way we could make all this work without your mom." Dad made sure we heard him giving her credit where it was due.

Mom's and Dad's schedules meant they had little time together. It seemed more like they were just crossing paths, but the way they took care of the four of us has left a lasting impression on me. I carry so much of their influence with me in my day-to-day life, especially, I hope, as a parent.

Dad was a humble man—probably humble to a fault. Like many other war veterans, he never talked about his combat days. When the Japanese bombed Pearl Harbor, Dad walked away from his football scholarship to enlist in the Marines. It wasn't until 2002, when my dad was eighty and on his deathbed, that I learned the incredible story of my dad's military service.

As Dad's time neared, a longtime friend named Bill Justice came to visit him in the hospital. Mr. Justice had grown up with my dad, and they'd played college football together. They also went to fight in the war at the same time, with my dad going to Japan and Mr. Justice going to Europe. Because Mr. Justice had served in World War II as well, Dad told him war stories he never told anyone else, including my mom.

I was standing next to Mr. Justice when he looked at Dad in his bed and said, "Well, Chizik, you made it fifty more years than you should have." I looked at Mr. Justice curiously. I had no idea what he was talking about.

When Mr. Justice left the room, I followed him out. "Mr. Justice," I asked, "what did you mean when you said he made it fifty more years than he should have?"

"Have you ever read about Sugar Loaf Hill?" Mr. Justice asked me.

"No," I replied.

"Have you ever even heard of Sugar Loaf Hill?"

"No."

Mr. Justice told me the story of this key stronghold in the Battle of Okinawa, one of the bloodiest battles of World War II. Tens of thousands of lives on both sides were lost there. From what I've been told, my dad was one of hundreds of men who went up Sugar Loaf Hill and one of only a dozen from his company who survived.

Dad received a Bronze Star for carrying a couple of wounded soldiers through serious artillery fire. As a kid, I would go into Dad's bedroom, dig through his drawers, pull out his Bronze

Star, and pin it on my shirt because I thought it was some kind of toy. It was in a black box that said *Bronze Star*, but I never knew what it meant until I heard the story from Mr. Justice. Dad had never said anything to us about it.

When I was coaching at Texas, ABC did a feature story on my dad at halftime of one of our games. I didn't get to see the story, but the following Monday I started receiving e-mail after e-mail about it.

One message was from a gentleman who had fought alongside my dad at Okinawa and had written notes every day of the battle. He sent me copies of his notes, and in them he told of a time during a cease-fire when he, my dad, and another soldier were sitting together chatting. All of a sudden, despite the cease-fire, they came under attack. They heard an incoming missile, and before they could scramble to a safer spot, the missile landed right next to my dad. It didn't explode. The missile was a dud.

Who knows how many other instances there were like that one where my dad narrowly escaped death the three and a half years he fought in the war. As I think about these stories, it hits me hard that if my dad had not been one of the few who survived Sugar Loaf Hill or if that missile hadn't been a dud, I wouldn't be here today. That perspective takes me back to my purpose. It gives me a feeling that I'm supposed to be here on earth. My being alive is no accident, and my being a football coach is no accident either. I have a purpose, and knowing how close I was to not being here motivates me to fulfill my calling. It has to be a God thing.

I've been asked how I can confidently stand up and face scrutiny and criticism as head coach when controversies and accusations have hit my programs. I have a two-part answer. First, even though it may not feel this way at times, being a head coach isn't that hard. What my dad experienced in the war, now that was hard. Second, I can keep my sense of purpose as I consider the instances when my father's life could have ended and how I'm alive only because he was spared each time. I believe I'm supposed to be here on this earth.

I recently attended a fund-raiser back home in Clearwater, and Mr. Justice was seated at my table. Shortly afterward he mailed me a letter. I've received probably close to ten letters from Mr. Justice since Dad passed away. He likes to mail me a letter after my coaching accomplishments, and invariably that letter will say something like "Your dad would never say it, but, boy, you know he would be really proud of you."

The letter he wrote me after the Clearwater event read:

Dear Gene,

It was really great to see you last Saturday. I appreciated being able to sit with you. I know that I've told you this before, but your dad would be real proud. He would never brag or boast, but I know that he would be proud. He would just sit there and tilt his head to the side and say, "He's pretty good, ain't he?"

9

....

OUR FOOTBALL FAMILY

FAITH IS NOT the only area of my life I have learned to blend with football. I've done the same with family.

We make it a priority to foster a family environment within our program, not only allowing coaches' families to attend practices and hang around with our players, but also making our families an intentional part of the program. As a result, our football team has become an extended family of sorts.

But before I talk to you about our Tigers family, I want to tell you about my family. This is outside the norm for me because I try to keep my family out of the spotlight as much as possible. I think it's important to keep a barrier in place around my kids, so I rarely talk to the media about my personal life.

College football brings deep-seated passion out of fans. When that passion is channeled in the proper manner, it's a wonderful thing. The pageantry of game day on a college campus is something no other level of football and no other sport can match. You can't imagine what it's like to do a Tiger Walk, where thousands of fans pat us on the back and cheer us on as we pass by. Then to go inside the stadium and hear the almost-deafening roar of eighty-eight thousand fans cheering for us as we take the field for the game . . . it's an incredibly emotional experience.

Even going on the road and playing in front of a stadium full of fans rooting against us is a welcome feeling in a curious sort of way. I don't think anyone honestly prefers being jeered over being cheered, but there's something about going into an opponent's stadium where the fans are booing you and hoping to see you fail that brings you closer as a team.

The fans' game day passion, whether for you or against you, drives you during the week. Playing to win for your fans falls into that category of getting outside yourself and realizing that you are playing and coaching for a much larger group. At the end of the game, both teams and the entire stadium can look up at the big scoreboard and see who won that day. Sometimes the outcome matches your performance; sometimes it doesn't. But either way, the final score is what you're judged by.

And that's where the flip side of passion can come in. While the energy from fans can be motivating, it can also be misdirected. That's why Jonna and I believe it's so important to try to protect our children.

I am a college football coach. That is the profession I have chosen. But that is not my identity. I am Gene Chizik, husband of Jonna and father to Kennedy, Landry, and Cally. That is who I am. That is my true identity. Fans lose sight of that, though.

We definitely make that distinction to our children and to

everyone else we come in contact with, but sometimes that line is difficult for fans to draw. Most only see me as Coach Chizik. The problem with that is then I get treated in direct proportion to how many wins my team has. If I have good records and win bowl games, I get treated great. If I have losing seasons and miss bowl games, I don't.

That's why I constantly emphasize to my children, "Being a coach is not who I am; it's just what I do." It's difficult to get that point across, though, because our thirteen-year-olds and our eleven-year-old have a hard time separating the two when someone at school talks to them about Auburn football and their father. This is when it becomes very personal to them. It can be hard on our children when their classmates repeat negative comments they've heard at home.

Those types of things are tough to hear when you're a kid, and it's a nonstop uphill battle for us. Jonna and I are adults, and we know that people can make statements they don't really mean. But Kennedy, Landry, and Cally don't get that yet.

There have been many family discussions and bedtime chats about this topic in the Chizik household. I even do role-playing with the kids. If we lose on a Saturday, on Sunday night before they go to bed, I'll say something to them like "Okay, I'm Johnny walking down the hall at school tomorrow. Johnny says to you sarcastically, 'Great job. Auburn stinks. Your dad blew it. Landry, Kennedy—nice game.'" The kids will then give me their response—if there is one to be made—and I'll guide them as needed in preparation for the next day at school. I try to make it as lighthearted as possible, but I want to alert them so that when those comments are made, our kids are ready.

What I would hope to communicate to fans of any team is

this: Draw a clear line for yourself in your sports passions. If you want to be critical of a coach or his team, that's fine as long as your comments are within reason. It's part of the game; I know that. But if you happen to be around kids whose parents are coaches at any level, be mindful that they're kids and they're not as experienced as you are, so word your criticisms around them carefully, if at all.

You can be disappointed with a game's outcome or a team's season, but don't cross the line so the coach's kids hear you as criticizing their father. And if you have children who attend school with a coach's kids, have this discussion with them. Teach them where that line is, and demonstrate to them with your words and actions how to keep the distinction between a team's coach and their friend's father.

Believe me when I say it gets a little crazy sometimes. I've received several death threats during my football career. When I hear one on my voice mail, I just hope it's from a fan of a different school rather than my own!

Please don't get me wrong. Football has been great for my family. I love college football so much I've made it my life's profession. It has provided financial security for us, and it has created opportunities we wouldn't have had otherwise, including being able to talk with Presidents Barack Obama, George W. Bush, and Bill Clinton and meeting some big stars, which our kids love.

There are times, though, when I sit down and weigh the sacrifices we've had to make as a family because of football. For one thing, we have surrendered privacy since I became a head coach. Even on family vacations, it's not easy to join the kids on the beach because someone will invariably recognize me and start snapping photos or capturing video of our family, or they'll shout something rude or obnoxious in our direction.

Family meals out have become much harder to pull off too. One time I took Cally to lunch after his baseball game. He left his seat to go to the restroom, and this fan must have been waiting for his opportunity because as soon as Cally left, this guy slid right into Cally's spot in the booth. "You don't mind if I sit here for a minute, do you?" the guy asked. My thought was *Of course I do.* But the fan immediately started in with "I had to talk to you about how the offense is looking and how the defense is doing."

It's endearing to see how our kids try to take care of me in their own way. Our daughters are especially protective of me. There have been times when I'm engaging with a group of fans in public, and Kennedy and Landry will come up to me, grab my arm, and say, "Come on, Daddy, we've gotta go. We're gonna be late." Or when we're looking for a place to eat, they'll scout out a restaurant while I wait in the car. If they see a table in the back where we can have some privacy, they'll ask for it and motion for me to come on in. If there are no tables available in a quiet area, they'll return to the car and say, "We need to go somewhere else."

They take all those steps because in those few moments I have with my family, I'm not Coach Chizik; I'm Gene, Jonna's husband, and Kennedy, Landry, and Cally's dad.

BEFORE IT'S TOO LATE

My daughters are thirteen now. I know that the teenage years are a crucial time for girls to have a strong father presence in their lives. My biggest fear since my girls were born has been that my job would not allow me to be around them as much as I need to be. So shortly after they were born, I started buying books about dads and daughters. I make concerted efforts to be involved in my daughters' lives as much as possible because I know that if girls don't feel secure in Daddy's love, they're going to find a replacement love somewhere else.

When the girls were really young, I started having individual date nights with them, and I still like to put on nice clothes and take them to a restaurant or do something special with them for daddy-daughter time. I enjoy those events with them, and our date nights also allow me to show my daughters how they should expect to be treated when they start dating.

I pray with my girls each night before they go to bed. During that time I also talk to them about school. One thing I'm intentional about is learning their friends' names, because it's important to young girls that Dad knows who their friends are and keeps up with the relationships they have at school.

I've always driven the girls to school in the mornings. They only recently asked, "Dad, you bring us to school every day. Why?"

My answer was "Because it's twenty-five minutes I can have with you every morning that I can't get any other time."

Sometimes when I'm able to take them home from school, I'll drive a longer way back just to steal a few more minutes with them. To a daughter, her dad's time with her equals love. I tell Kennedy and Landry how much it hurts me that I can't be around them as much as I wish I could. I want them to know that their daddy absolutely loves them and is committed to being part of their lives.

I have tried to make it extremely clear to all my children that if my job ever came between me and them, I would go lay asphalt tomorrow. My daughters and I have recently had some candid

Here I am in 1971 (age nine), right before my first game with the Clearwater Cyclones.

This is my dad, Gene Chizik Sr., when he played for Rollins College in Orlando, Florida, back in 1941— just before he left to fight in World War II.

Playing catch with Dad at the nearby middle school in Clearwater

This is the only photo I have of my dad wearing his Bronze Star, awarded for his bravery during the Battle of Sugar Loaf Hill in World War II. Out of the hundreds of men who charged that hill, my dad was one of only a dozen from his company to make it back down.

◄ The football legacy
continues . . . me with
our son, Cally (age 2½),
at Jordan-Hare Stadium.

Our twin girls, Landry and Kennedy, were
born on October 25, 1997, just two hours
before the Stephen F. Austin–McNeese State
game–the biggest game of my career at the
time and one of the best days of my life.

Me, Jonna, Kennedy,
Landry, and Cally following
a victory celebration at
Toomer's Corner in 2004,
when I was Auburn's
defensive coordinator

The press conference
in 2008 when I was
introduced as Auburn's
new head football coach ▶

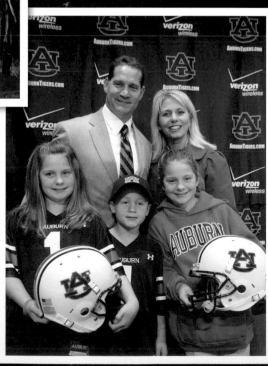

◄ Addressing the media upon my arrival at Auburn on December 14, 2008

▲ Doing the Tiger Walk before our game against South Carolina, September 25, 2010. War Eagle!

Coming out of the tunnel on September 4, 2010, in our season opener against Arkansas State ▶

Taking the field against Kentucky on October 9, 2010

Celebrating a touchdown against Arkansas on October 16, 2010

Giving a pep talk before our game against Mississippi State on September 9, 2010

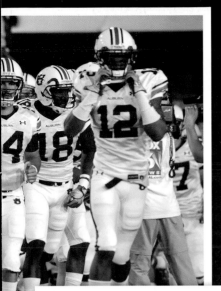

Jonna and me getting soaked by our players during a Family Fun Day at the water park in 2009

Getting soaked again following our 49–31 victory over Georgia in November 2010

◄ Cheering after our 28–27 victory over Alabama in the 2010 Iron Bowl

Praying with the team after our 62–24 victory over Chattanooga in November 2010

The Auburn faithful cheering us on at the National Championship Game in Glendale, Arizona, January 10, 2011 ▸

◂ With Cam Newton after our 1   ctory over Mississippi State, September 9, 2010

Wes Byrum (#18) and Neil Caudle (#19, on his back) celebrate after the winning field goal against Oregon.

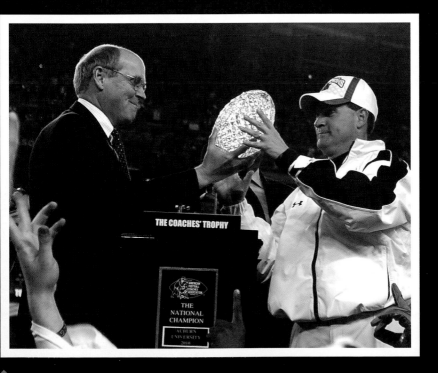

Accepting the Coaches' Trophy after defeating Oregon at the National Championship Game, January 10, 2011

Celebrating with Jonna at the end of a truly remarkable journey, January 10, 2011

conversations about the tension I feel between being a coach and being there for them. Without fail, Kennedy and Landry say, "Daddy, we love what you do. Don't give up coaching. We know you want to be around us." They say that because they know where my priorities are—with them.

As for Cally, he's my boy and he's always going to be my boy. He can come up to the athletic offices and go to practice and be around me as much as he wants. I love that he gets to be my locker room rat and that he gets to spend time there with me and the players.

Cally has also had to cope with my being a public figure. We went to a recent father-son breakfast at a local All Pro Dad function that is a part of Tony Dungy's outstanding program for training men to be better fathers. We had a little trouble leaving because of the number of people who came up to me and wanted to shake my hand or request an autograph. When we finally made our way out, Cally said, "Dad, I don't want you to go to another one of these." I asked him why not. He said, "I know you don't want to be doing all that stuff when you're spending time with me."

Goodness, that tore me up, because even at a fathering program, I was getting pulled away from my son. But on the other hand, I was able to hear Cally express his love for me in a way he might not have otherwise.

My job is a time and energy vampire. I spend a great deal of time trying to regulate so many people and so many different areas—cultivating this, managing that, being proactive about this. It sucks up all my time, and when I sacrifice time, I know that I'm taking away minutes that my family could have been getting with me.

An intense fear I've had is that I'll look up one day and see that the kids have grown up. I'll be at home and retired from coaching, but it'll be too late—they'll all be gone. That is why I'm always trying to get them to spend time with me at work, whether it's coming to a practice or having lunch on the deck outside my office. I want them here as much as possible. But I'm already seeing a difference as the kids are growing older. They have their friends, along with their own sports, school, and church activities, so their schedules are getting busier.

I pray constantly that I will find extra moments to spend time with them and that when we are all together, it will be quality, uninterrupted family time.

GAME TIME!

Because we are a football family, I'd like to share football-related stories involving each of the children.

First, the twins.

Kennedy and Landry were born on game day of what to that point was the biggest game of my coaching career. It was 1997, and I was defensive coordinator at Stephen F. Austin State University in the beautiful little city of Nacogdoches, Texas.

Ever since we found out Jonna was pregnant, we had joked that she was going to deliver the twins on a game day. About 2 or 3 a.m. on the day we were going to play McNeese State University, Jonna woke me up with a nudge.

"Gene," she said, "I think they're coming."

"Yeah, right." I rolled over to go back to sleep.

About ten minutes later I received a firm shove.

"Yeah, yeah, yeah," I said.

"No, Gene, I seriously think this is it."

I was a little annoyed that she was choosing to wake me up this early on the morning of our huge game just so she could enjoy a laugh.

"There's no way that you're having these kids today," I informed her. "There is no way."

She said, "I think I am. I think I am."

"If you are, then let's go."

Just like that, we were out of bed and headed to the hospital.

We met with the doctor, who was a friend of ours, and being the sensitive husband I am, I said, "Hey, Doc, is this for real? If so, we've either got to slow this down or speed this up because I've got a game coming up at one o'clock."

Not only was this a game day, but it was also a day game—not a night game, which would have bought me more time at the hospital. Plus, this was a huge game because we were about halfway through the season and both teams were undefeated and highly ranked nationally.

"Gene," the doctor notified me, "I think it's time."

"Well," I said to the doctor and Jonna, "y'all can't be waiting now. Y'all have got to either do it now or do it tonight. One or the other."

"Hey, we'll do it now," the doctor said.

"Doc, my game starts at one o'clock, and I've got to know that everyone's okay."

"We can get it done," he assured me.

Jonna had a C-section, and the girls were born around ten o'clock that morning. The babies were fine and Jonna was fine, and with kickoff approaching, Jonna told me, "Go."

With permission to leave granted, I ran to my car and booked it to the stadium. When I arrived, the team was already on the field for pregame warm-ups. I'd missed the team meal and stretching, but the players knew I was at the hospital with Jonna. I hurried onto the field, and Jeremiah Trotter, our outstanding linebacker who went on to play eleven seasons in the NFL, came up to me and said, "Coach, don't worry about it, baby." I think he knew I was stressed out. "We've got this one today."

We played perhaps the best defensive game of any team I've ever coached and won 13–7, keeping our perfect record.

I'll never forget that day.

John Pearce, our head coach, had called me at the hospital that morning to tell me, "You take care of those babies and your wife. Don't come back here until you're ready, because today's going to be a great day." Now that I'm a head coach, I can look back and appreciate Coach Pearce's words. His message to me was *Don't worry about the game. You've done your work all week to get us ready for this. Now just take care of your family.*

He was right about it being a great day, but the incredible thing is how little I remember from the game. I recall being up in the press box and calling defenses as the defensive coordinator, and I remember how well our defense played. I know it was an overflow crowd at our stadium and the place was going nuts, but that's about it. Usually a coach can recite almost an entire play-by-play of a game, especially one as big as that game. But my mind was such a blur from Kennedy and Landry's birth that that's about all I can recall from that day.

I do remember, though, rushing back to the hospital as soon as the game ended. I remember holding my kids in my arms and thinking, *Man, this is as good as it gets. This is as awesome as it gets.*

As I said, that was the biggest game of my life to that point, but looking back, the game seems so small compared to the rest of that day. A whole new world opened up for me that morning. My twin daughters were born, and I became a dad. That was a rush no football win could come close to.

WHAT'S IN A NAME

My son's full name is Eugene Calloway Chizik III. His first name is a tribute to my dad's legacy, and his middle name is a tribute to one of my former players.

Calloway Belcher was an outstanding player for us at Stephen F. Austin. He was a defensive back when I first arrived there in 1992, and we struck up an immediate bond. After the 1993 season, we moved him to linebacker, which was the position I coached. Cally, as everyone called him, had the complete package anyone would hope for in a young man: smart and disciplined academically, a tough football player but polite off the field, good looking, and unassumingly confident. He represented himself, his family, and our school the best way possible in everything he did.

He was, in short, what you would want your son to be when you send him off to college.

During spring practices in March 1994, between his junior and senior seasons, Cally took a hit to his helmet. As he was walking toward the sideline, he collapsed. When I saw what had happened, I ran over to him. The team doctor was kneeling beside him, and I could see panic in the doctor's eyes. This was back before we carried cell phones, so the doctor ordered someone to run to a phone and call 911.

I arrived at the hospital shortly after the ambulance. Cally had suffered a brain aneurysm and was in a coma. His parents were called and had to drive two hours to be with their only son, who now was basically brain dead. I remember thinking, *I can't even imagine having this happen to my only son. They turned him loose to play college football, and now they get a phone call and have to drive to see their son, who is all but dead. How did this happen? How did this go wrong? Where did this take a bad turn?* I remained at the hospital waiting for Cally's parents to arrive, thinking, *How do you deal with this as a parent?*

I can still see the complete shock on his parents' faces when they first walked into Cally's room and saw their son lying in the bed. I wasn't married yet and hadn't experienced what it's like to have a child or to know how deeply a parent can love a child. But the looks on their faces said it all.

Cally never regained consciousness, and a week after his final practice, at age twenty-two, he passed away. His death took the wind out of my sails. It seemed so needless. I had watched him play a game that is supposed to be fun, and it killed him.

I've never felt as low as a coach as I did then. Before Cally passed away, I had sat alone in the hospital, trying to come to grips with what was happening, and thinking, *If I ever have a son, I want him to be like Cally.*

I decided that when I had my first son, he'd go by Cally. Our Cally was born six years later when I was at Central Florida. I called the Belchers and told them, "I want to let you know that I'd like to name our son Cally in remembrance of your Cally. Would you be okay with that?" They gave us their blessing, and my only son is a reminder to me that life is precious and nothing about the length of our lives is guaranteed.

I also think about Cally Belcher every time we recruit a player. College football has become a big business, a multimillion-dollar entertainment industry. It's easy for coaches to temporarily lose touch with what these players really mean to us on a day in, day out basis because of all the pressure we are under to win. But because of Cally, one of the points we make to recruits' parents is that we will never forget that every recruit is someone's son.

My own son's name won't let me forget.

10

EXTENDING THE FAMILY

BY MY ESTIMATE, 60 percent of our players come from single-parent homes.

The word *family* gets thrown around a lot among sports teams, but for our team it is more than a cliché. We truly consider ourselves a family.

This comes with a challenge, though, when well over half of our players have never experienced being a member of a strong family unit. If they haven't been part of a cohesive family at home, how can they be expected to know how to function as a family in the locker room or on the playing field?

That's why I am adamant that our coaches' families be a part of our football program. Our coaches' families don't merely model for our players what a family unit should be; they actively participate in making our football team a family. We treat the Auburn football players as our extended family of sorts.

Every Sunday night during the season we have team dinners, and our families join us for these events. The coaches' wives and kids come and eat with us, regardless of whether we won or lost the previous day.

Our coaches' families come to practices and spend time in the athletic offices with us too. I want our players to see me and the rest of the staff not just as coaches but also as husbands and fathers. A number of our coaches have young boys and girls, and during practices the kids may be running around the goalpost or tossing footballs back and forth. The kids can get a little loud with their playing sometimes, but our players just have to learn to work around it. It's worth it to me to have them see those parent-child interactions firsthand.

It does make for some interesting mishaps, though—like the practice leading up to last season's BCS Championship Game. There we were, right in the middle of practice, preparing for a chance to win the national championship, when one of the players said to me, "Hey, Coach, do you have a white golden retriever?"

"Yeah," I said. "But why are you talking about retrievers right now?"

"Well," he said, "that's probably your dog running around over there with the defense."

I looked over to that part of the field, and sure enough, Lacy, our dog, was interfering with our defense's practice. My daughters had accidentally turned Lacy loose and were trying to catch her. Finally Lacy did stop . . . to poop on our practice field. The players got a kick out of that.

Yes, things can get more complicated when you bring kids and dogs to practices, but it's worth it when you consider all the benefits for both the players and the families.

We want our players to become good fathers and husbands, but what good would it do if we stood up in team meetings and emphasized the importance of marriage and fatherhood but didn't give them concrete examples of how a good father and husband looks, talks, and acts? My marriage isn't perfect—it can't be because I'm a part of it!—but it is a loving, biblically centered marriage. Jonna is around our team enough that she should probably demand to be on the payroll, which means the players can see how she and I communicate and get along with each other in our marriage.

Jonna and our other coaches' wives also play a motherly role for our players by doing things like handing out meals to them after games. That might sound like a small thing, but it's not. The players are starving after games, and usually student trainers and student managers make sure they get a postgame meal. But Jonna and other coaches' wives jump in and help distribute the food to the guys. Along with the meals, our wives will give them a postgame hug, win or lose, and that serves as a tangible reminder to them that the results of the game don't define them. Regardless of how the game came out or how a player performed, a mom is there to give him a hug that says, *You're loved unconditionally.*

Another benefit to the wives' handing out meals is that the players see them living what we preach: that we weren't put on this earth to be served, but to serve.

Just as my dad would acknowledge to my sisters and me our mom's vital role in our family, I try to give Jonna her due credit whenever I can.

By now you can probably imagine how much slack Jonna has to pick up for me at home due to my schedule. For six or seven months of the year, I'm sure she feels like a single mom. But despite the time demands my job places on her, she still somehow finds time to take on a motherly role with our players. We should probably give her a "Coach Mom" title or something like that.

Coaching is, after all, in her blood.

I told you there's an interesting story of how Jonna and I got together. I was in high school and she was in elementary school when we first met. That gets people's attention when they ask about our story! So it wasn't love at first sight for us. Not for me, anyway—you'll have to ask Jonna whether she had a young schoolgirl's crush on me at the time.

Jonna's father was my high school's head football coach. I jokingly say that my first memory of her was as a snotty-nosed, bratty, pigtailed kid with dirty feet running around our field house.

Then, ten years after I graduated high school, when I was coaching at Middle Tennessee State, I went back home to Clearwater during Christmas break and met this pretty blonde one night.

When we exchanged names, I said, "I'm Gene Chizik."

"Gene Chizik?" she asked.

"Yeah," I said.

An *aha* look lit up her face. "I know you," she said. "I'm Coach Nicely's daughter. You're on my wall at home."

Her dad had placed photos of his team captains in the hallway of their family home. She told me she walked past my picture every time she passed through her hall growing up.

"So you're Jonna?" I asked, still stunned.

"Yes, Jonna Nicely."

Whoa, I thought. *You're kidding me.*

The next question I asked her was "How old are you?"

"Twenty-two," she answered.

Phew!

She was all grown up now, a graduate of Florida State—not snotty-nosed, bratty, or pigtailed. And best I could tell, she had clean feet.

"Hey, why don't you come over during break and say hello to my folks?" she asked.

"I don't think I can do that," I told her. "You're my head coach's daughter."

But Jonna and I must have been meant to be together. We started long-distance dating, then after just two or three months, I took a job at Stephen F. Austin. Jonna landed a job at SFA, too, running an all-girls dorm while she took additional classes for a teaching degree. We kept dating, and in June 1996, we became Mr. and Mrs. Gene Chizik.

Fifteen years later, we are the proud parents of Kennedy, Landry, and Cally . . . and 120-plus players on the Auburn football team.

WE'RE ALL FAMILY

Having our families actively involved in the program allows our players to see us both disciplining and loving on our children. When I stand up and discuss kindergarten rules or character issues in team meetings, I can say, "I'm not telling you anything different from what I would tell my son, Cally." And they can relate to that because they know Cally. They see the two of us in the office and on the practice field together as father and son.

I'll talk in team meetings about my daughters and our expectations for them as they grow up to become young women. The players soak up those talks because they know Kennedy and Landry and they see me hug my girls and put my arms around them at practice. We want the players to see how to properly treat a female, whether it's their girlfriends, their wives, or their mothers.

But the role modeling goes both ways, as we expect the players to be examples for our children too. We teach them that they are basically older siblings to our kids. That puts responsibility on them to act, speak, and behave in a manner that sets a good example for the next generation. When our kids are around, we don't want the players walking around with their pants sagging. If I see one of the players with his pants too low, I'll tell him, "I've got two thirteen-year-old daughters, and I don't want them to see that." Up come their pants.

Being role models for kids is part of the players' duties. We remind them that no matter where they go, kids are watching how they act. Even when our kids aren't around—if the guys head over to other parts of campus or to restaurants around town—someone is always paying attention, whether they realize it or not.

The players have spectacular relationships with our kids. I'll look off to the side during practices and see players interacting on the sideline with Cally or Kennedy or Landry or one of the other coaches' kids, and as much as I like a structured and efficient practice, I realize that those spontaneous moments benefit both our players and our kids.

It's all part of what we mean when we say we're family.

THE CIRCLE

One of the ways we strengthen and protect our football family is through the concepts of "the circle" and "impostors."

We draw a figurative circle with the players, coaching staff, our families, and athletic department personnel on the inside.

We find validation only from those within the circle. Although we respect all those outside our circle, we do not have the time or energy to worry about everyone's opinion.

This isn't an elitist mentality. Instead, it's a way to protect ourselves. We are a family, and family members take care of each other. That's why we don't allow anyone into our circle who intends to harm one of our own physically, emotionally, or spiritually. Anyone who is brought into the group must seek out the best for the members of our football family. We talk about this circle—who's in and who's not—a great deal.

Sometimes we talk with players about the circle concept when we need to communicate truth to them about their friendships outside of football. As family members, it's our responsibility to watch out for each other and not allow a teammate to spend too much time with bad influences who hinder his ability to make wise choices. When players make poor choices, it affects the entire team—everyone within the circle. Our guys know that, which is why there's such a strong "Watch out for your brother" mind-set in our program.

It's a lot like a biological family. If a child gets in trouble at school, he's not just reflecting poorly on himself. He's also negatively impacting everyone who carries his name. Being a part of a family carries with it a responsibility to reflect well on others in the family . . . and a responsibility to prevent others from making unwise decisions, too.

To me personally, the circle means not seeking validation from outside sources. My measure of success as a coach is to run our program the right way and stick to that plan. Because I have established who I am in Christ and in my relationships with my family and the guys in our program, the outside attacks don't affect me.

If I tried to lead my program based on message boards, blogs, and everybody else who has an opinion, this job would quickly eat me alive. I pray constantly for peace, knowing that my character, my integrity, my manhood, and all the things that I stand for will at some point come under attack. I know those darts and arrows will come. But when they hit me, by the grace of God they simply bounce off. He gives me a shield of peace to protect me from those attacks. I'm convinced I couldn't make it in this profession without the strength God provides.

In addition to the circle, we also talk in our program about impostors, which is a concept I took from Mack Brown at Texas. Impostors are circumstances that distort reality, for better or worse, and they show up both in football and in the outside world. During a game, we'll caution our players about the impostors that can show up on our sideline when we're leading 21–0. Or when we're trailing 21–0. We can be up by three touchdowns, but maybe we're not playing twenty-one points better than our opponent. Maybe we've struggled on offense, but our opponent made a couple of big mistakes on their end of the field and we converted a couple of turnovers into easy points. If we're not playing well but believe what the scoreboard is telling us, we run the risk of becoming complacent and watching those opportunities for easy points evaporate. If we fall for what the impostors are saying, before long that 21–0 lead is gone and we've lost all momentum . . . and eventually the game, too.

Impostors can also work in the other direction. A 21–0 deficit doesn't have to mean that the game is lost. Maybe a couple of bad bounces went against us. If we keep playing well, we can wipe out that three-touchdown lead and have a chance to win the game. But if we believe the impostor—that 21–0 deficit we supposedly can't overcome—we lose all hope of winning a game that could have been within our grasp.

The only score that really matters is the one on the board when the clock reads 0:00. That's the final product, the real deal.

Impostors show up in the outside world, too, where sometimes the things you see, read, and hear are not necessarily what they seem. Unfortunately, once something is in print, it becomes gospel to many people. And in this era of blogs and social media, anyone can print anything, whether it contains partial truth or any truth at all. Once the public forms an opinion about a certain person or situation, it becomes really hard to change that perception. That's the power of the pen . . . or the keyboard.

We can't control what is said about us, but we can try to prevent those within our circle from letting impostors define how we think about ourselves. We tell the players that they're going to read negative things on message boards, they're going to hear negative talk on the radio, and they're going to read negative opinions in print. We tell them that paying attention to the negative things being said about them is like drinking poison. "Unless it comes from us," I tell the players, "it's not real. Consider it an impostor."

That's one of the reasons it's so crucial for me to earn the players' trust by always being open and honest with them. If there's something that needs to be said, I tell it to the players immediately. It's always better to hear a tough truth from someone who's on your side, someone who's saying it out of love, than from someone outside the circle.

As head coach, I do my best to set our team on the right course and keep us there. Then I ask for God's peace to guard me and guide me—to guide all of us.

WHEN THINGS GO WRONG

Discipline is part of a family too.

Not long after I started working on this book, four of our players were arrested and charged with robbery, burglary, and theft.

Our preference, obviously, is that our program would avoid making such embarrassing headlines. I don't know if that's possible, but I firmly believe that we do everything we can to keep players out of trouble. Still, trouble happens.

When it does, for all of us behind the scenes, it's emotionally devastating. We go through the full gamut of emotions, asking ourselves a range of what-if questions: *What if I had said this?* Or *What if I had done this?* Because of the family concept we have in the Auburn football program, it feels as though our own child has gotten into trouble.

Here's my take on situations like these: anything related to our program that becomes an embarrassment, a character issue, or a problem is my fault. I'm the head coach; I'm in charge of every one of the more than two hundred people connected to Auburn football. I can't control what each person does every day and every night, but it comes with my title to accept the responsibility when anyone under my charge brings shame to our team or university.

In the case of the four players who were arrested, I took immediate action by removing them from the team that day. My statement to the media gives insight into my feelings about these types of problems:

"The players arrested in connection with this deeply troubling incident have been permanently dismissed from our football team. While we realize the legal process will run its course and these young men have a right for their case to be heard, playing for Auburn University is an honor and a privilege. It is not a right. We hold our student-athletes to a high standard of conduct on and off the field as representatives of Auburn University, and this kind of behavior is not tolerated.

"I am extremely disappointed and embarrassed by the actions of these individuals. I want to personally apologize to all of those who were impacted by this senseless act, including the victims, Auburn University, and the Auburn family."

That was a painful day for me as CEO of Auburn football.

We try, just as we did with our Iowa State program, to go over and above what's required in educating the players about ethics and acceptable behavior. During our freshman meetings, we address all kinds of social pressures and athletic pressures that players face. We are proactive when it comes to topics like alcohol and illegal drugs. We point out potential for trouble, on campus and off. We go over everything that could become an NCAA violation, including having an agent, accepting money, and receiving forbidden contributions and gifts. We get down to the nitty-gritty details, such as an alum walking into a restaurant and saying to a player, "Let me pay for that meal for you." That can't happen, and we explain to players why not.

We bring in motivational and inspirational speakers. I'm constantly talking to athletes about how to make wise decisions. We have hired coaches with a unique knack for serving as role models and mentoring players. We even go outside of coaching assignments at times to try to find the right fit for specific players.

Within every team, however, there will be what we call "edge players"—guys who are closest to the edge of trouble. They are the ones we have to make sure we're on top of so they don't go in the wrong direction. A player may be on the edge for a number of reasons—because of how he grew up, because of his home life, because of his family background, because of the crowd he hung out with in high school. We identify who our edge players are and devote extra time and attention to them. We do whatever we can to be on the front end of trouble. We'll have these guys spend time at coaches' houses, especially on Friday and Saturday nights when they could potentially find trouble.

Our players know that we have high standards here. The truth is that if a player enjoys being at Auburn, he will live within our standards. I don't consider my philosophy to be a no-tolerance policy because that makes it sound like I don't issue second chances. I do when the circumstances warrant one. But if a player doesn't adhere to our standards, he won't be here. There's no gray area.

With the arrested players, they obviously didn't fall in line with our standards. As a result, I did not have a decision to make as to whether they would remain a part of our program. They made that decision themselves.

Whenever we have players get into trouble, it shines a spotlight on our program's recruiting process. Not every decision we make is perfect, but we do our best to recruit the right players. We do as much homework on recruits up front as we can. We talk to their parents, their coaches, their teachers—anyone who can share information with us. Recruiting is not an exact science, and we like to collect as much information as possible. I don't care if a recruit has a five-star rating; all it takes is for one of our coaches to say he has character issues or he's not the right fit for Auburn, and that player's name is off our list.

There are recruits we know are edge players. But as we recruit them, we think, *We believe we can change them. We can get them going in the right direction.* I measure recruits by their hearts. Maybe we're looking at a guy who grew up with a really hard life. Maybe he didn't have a dad around, or his mother might have been in and out of prison. But what I'm thinking about as I determine whether this recruit could become an Auburn player is, *Is his heart right? Does he have a great spirit about him? When you talk to his teachers, do they say, "He works really hard and I love having him in my class"? Does the principal say, "You know, he's had a rough life, and based on where he's come from, it's amazing that he's able to do what he does"?*

We're confident in our program, and the percentage of edge players who end up being successful here is extremely high. Our goal is to have our guys graduate and go into society as great citizens, and in the majority of cases I feel like we do this quite well. But there will always be that small percentage we don't get through to like we want to.

Whether you're leading a football program or a corporation, you have to realize that you can guide people as far as the day is long, but you can't make decisions for them. Each person must make his own decisions, and each person must then be held accountable for the consequences of those decisions.

When I have players who get into trouble, my most painful moment is calling their parents. When someone in our program makes a poor choice that is going to negatively affect him for the rest of his life, I tell our coaches, "We tried all we could with him. Let's just make sure right now that we don't kick the parents to the curb. Let's make sure we're riding with the parents through this."

I hate feeling like we have let the parents down. We told them during the recruiting process that we would take care of their son and that we'd have his best interests in mind. As coaches we have visited with recruits' families, and we've learned the backstories of parents who worked multiple jobs to provide for their children or who made sacrifices on the outside chance that their son could become one of the 2 percent of high school athletes to earn an athletic scholarship.

And now, as a result of one bad decision, that boy has caused hurt for both his families—his biological family and his football family—and most important, for himself. As painful as these situations are for the Auburn team, my hope is that they can serve as learning opportunities—both for the players who made the choice and for their teammates who are on the sideline watching.

11

TRUST TEST

IT WAS A HINGE MOMENT for our program.

We were three weeks from our 2009 season opener against Louisiana Tech. For eight months our almost entirely new coaching staff had been working hard to lay the foundation for this new era of Auburn football. The players were responding well to the sweeping changes we had made, and the old walls of division within the team were gradually crumbling.

We weren't to the point of complete trust I had promised in the first meeting, but we were making progress. And this moment in the team meeting room, with my first game as Auburn's head coach fast approaching, would swing the door of trust in one of two directions.

Junior Kodi Burns stepped front and center to address his teammates. No one made a sound as he cleared his throat. Every player in our program was there, anxious to hear what Kodi had to say. So were the coaches. So was I.

Auburn had been plagued by a quarterback controversy throughout much of its 5–7 season in 2008, and from what I had been told, it became one of the most divisive issues on a team already fractured by tensions.

Kodi had started seven games as quarterback in 2008; Chris Todd had started the other five. Kodi was a prized high school recruit who had been brought on two years earlier by an offensive coordinator who had since been fired; Chris was a junior college transfer brought in for the 2008 season by the next offensive coordinator, Tony Franklin. Kodi was African American; Chris was white. There were ingredients in the mix that could prove to be a recipe for disaster.

To further complicate matters, players had chosen sides over which quarterback they believed should start. As the offense struggled to consistently score points, a division developed between offense and defense. In three conference games during the previous season, the defense had held opponents to seventeen points or fewer, but the team still lost. Fingers from the defensive side of the ball pointed across the line of scrimmage to the offense. And everyone had an opinion about who should be throwing the ball: Kodi or Chris.

Our coaching staff had a critical choice to make: who would be our starting quarterback? Just as important as our decision would be how we communicated that decision. We hadn't earned the players' complete trust yet. They were still evaluating us, just as we were still evaluating them.

We had to convince our players that this quarterback call wasn't about Kodi or Chris. This was about Auburn football.

We wouldn't give an ounce of consideration to how the two had arrived at Auburn. It wouldn't matter who the players favored. Nothing outside of football would influence our choice. We would pick the quarterback who would win the most games for the Auburn Tigers. That was the only factor.

Chris had missed all of spring practice because of shoulder surgery, so we hadn't been able to fully evaluate him until the summer. In the second week of August, after waiting about as long as we could, we made our decision.

We chose Chris over Kodi.

I told the coaches that offensive coordinator Gus Malzahn and I would call all the quarterbacks into my office and explain to each of them individually how we had reached our decision. After that we would meet with the team and inform the players. Then we would release the news to the media and be done with it.

Chris, naturally, was excited by the news. "You're gonna be our guy," I told him. "We feel like you give us the best chance to win, based on what we've seen. You worked for it, and we feel good about this move. We're going to announce it to everybody in the team meeting, we'll announce it to the media, and then we'll move on."

Next I called Kodi into my office. There was an anxious look on his face.

"Kodi," I began, "we're going to go in a different direction."

This was true on more levels than Kodi might have guessed. Not only were we pulling Kodi from starting quarterback, but we were also planning to move him to a different position altogether: receiver. In other words, Kodi would not be our backup quarterback. We didn't need Chris looking over his shoulder at a former starter who was ready to replace him as soon as the coach gave the signal. Besides, Kodi was a tremendous athlete, and we knew he could make our offense better by being on the field. But it wouldn't be at the position he preferred.

"We'd love for you to be a wideout," I told him. "We think you can help our team win. In our opinion, if you have a chance to go to the NFL after this, your best opportunity will be as wideout, and that's what we'd like you to play. I know this is really difficult for you to swallow. I don't want you to transfer. There are a thousand teams out there you could play quarterback for. But I want you at Auburn. We'll do something special here, and I want you to stay with us. You're good for this team and you're good for this locker room, and we need you at Auburn."

Kodi's look had become more distant as I talked. He was crushed.

"Yes, sir," he said, then left my office.

Would you like to guess the first person Kodi went to after leaving my office? Chette Williams, the team chaplain. I don't know how Chette counseled him, but it wasn't long before Kodi was back in my office. It appeared to me that he had been crying.

Kodi had one question he wanted to ask me. "Coach, can I talk to the team?"

"You got it," I answered.

We went to the meeting room to inform the players of our decision. I never asked Kodi what he intended to say.

"Chris is going to be our starter," I announced to the players. "There will be no team division. There will be no discussion. There will be no 'My friend should have gotten the position.' We're all on board and moving forward. This story will have headlines for one day, and then we're moving on. This is the choice. You need to trust us."

When I concluded, I nodded to Kodi, and he stood up. Every set of eyeballs in the room locked on him in anticipation.

"This is really hard for me today," he began. "But you know what? I don't want this to split our team up. I don't want there to be any discussion. I trust the coaches. If this is what they want us to do, this is what we're gonna do. I'm here to help us win games, and that's what I want to do. I'm not gonna lie—this hurts me. But you know what? I'm gonna do what the coaches ask me to do."

Ben Tate, our senior starting running back, stood up immediately after Kodi finished. Ben had experienced the problems caused by the previous year's quarterback controversy. "Nothing's gonna divide this team," he said resolutely. "I don't wanna hear any talking about anybody's opinion about it. We're moving ahead. The coaches have made their decision. We trust them to do the right thing. We're all moving forward now."

Looking back, I think the reason Kodi handled the situation in such an exemplary way was because he hadn't come here to play quarterback at Auburn. He had come here to play *football* at Auburn. The team door had swung in the direction of trust.

A WINNING STREAK

We opened the season at home against Louisiana Tech, and I was fired up during my first pregame Tiger Walk as head coach. I was at the back of the line, behind all the players, and I was pumping my fists and waving my arms to get the fans even more excited than they already were. My suit was drenched by the time I reached the stadium entrance. I was so ready to get this game started.

Interestingly enough, our first touchdown of the game—and the season—was scored by Kodi Burns. We had moved him to receiver, but we also decided to use him as a running quarterback out of our Wildcat formation near the opposing team's goal line. Kodi scored on a one-yard run to give us a 10–7 lead in the first quarter. When asked by the media after the game about Kodi's touchdown, I said, "Good things happen to good people." I thought it was appropriate that a guy who had put team first scored our team's first touchdown.

Chris played well too. He set a school record with a ninety-three-yard touchdown pass to Terrell Zachery in the third quarter, and he followed that up with another touchdown pass in the fourth quarter. We won our first game 37–13.

The next week we beat Mississippi State 49–24 in our first conference game. We got out to a 14–0 lead in the first quarter before falling behind 17–14 in the second. After that, though, we scored four unanswered touchdowns going into the fourth quarter and ended up winning 49–24. Kodi accounted for four touchdowns out of the Wildcat formation—three on one-yard runs and one on a pass to Philip Lutzenkirchen.

After one of Kodi's touchdowns I noticed that the first player from our sideline to meet him coming off the field was Chris. As Chris gave his teammate a big hug and congratulated him, I felt a sense of satisfaction. Even better than getting another touchdown was seeing the friction between teammates being eased.

In our third game, a nonconference matchup against West Virginia, we fell behind 14–0 in the first five minutes. We fought hard to come back, but it wasn't until early in the fourth quarter that we were able to take the lead for the first time at 34–30.

We added another touchdown late to win 41–30, bringing our record to 3–0. Chris threw four touchdowns in that game.

The next week, in a 54–30 victory over Ball State, Chris one-upped himself by throwing a school record–tying five touchdown passes. We had won our first four games, all at home.

Our fifth game would be a big test—a conference game at Tennessee with more than 102,000 fans in the Volunteers' stadium. We had trailed in each of our four wins, but we were never behind against Tennessee. Early in the fourth quarter we were ahead 23–6. Tennessee scored on the final play of the game, after we had already secured the victory, bringing the final score to 26–22.

It was five games into the season, and we had won five games. That matched the number of games Auburn had won the previous year and also the number of victories in my two seasons at Iowa State.

We would be back on the road again the following weekend to face Arkansas, which was 2–2 overall and had lost its first two SEC games. With our 5–0 record, we were going into Arkansas as a nationally ranked team for the first time all season. The Associated Press had us seventeenth in its poll, and we were number nineteen in the *USA Today* coaches' rankings.

When a team is 5–0, players start believing they're really good. We coaches, however, know that the film never lies. We watched game film for fourteen hours some days, and based on what the film was showing us, we knew we weren't a great team. We saw how we needed to improve in just about every area. We also knew that of the five teams we had defeated, only one had won more games than it had lost at that point in the season. We couldn't afford to get cocky as we looked ahead to our next game.

Arkansas might have been 2–2, but the Razorbacks had played a tough schedule. They had scored forty-one or more points in three of their games, and they were averaging almost 450 yards per game on offense. Plus, it doesn't matter what your opponent's record is—it's a chore to win any SEC game on the road.

Impostors. They'll get you every time when you start buying what they're selling you.

A LOSING STREAK

Arkansas and the impostors got us. We self-destructed early in the game, and the Razorbacks jumped to a 27–3 lead at halftime. Our deficit grew to 34–3 early in the third quarter before we finally started moving the ball on offense. We scored three straight touchdowns to get back into the game at 34–23, but we weren't able to score again. Arkansas added a touchdown and a field goal in the fourth quarter to beat us 44–23.

It was a sloppy game for the Tigers. We committed three turnovers, including a fumbled kickoff. We gave up a long kickoff return. We committed six penalties on defense, including three for pass interference. As a result, we no longer had an unbeaten record, and we lost our spots in the national rankings.

We returned home to face Kentucky, another team that was better than its record. Kentucky had lost three games in a row after starting 2–0, but all three of those losses came against ranked teams within our conference.

It was a chilly night with a problematic off-and-on wind. Both defenses played well, and our own defense carried us through the first three quarters. One of our touchdowns came on the return of a blocked field goal attempt in the first quarter, and that score looked like it would be the difference maker. We started the fourth quarter ahead 14–7, but Kentucky scored two touchdowns in the final seven minutes of the game to beat us 21–14. It was our first loss to Kentucky since 1966.

From our 5–0 start we had slipped to 5–2. Now we were entering the toughest stretch of our schedule, starting with a game at ninth-ranked LSU, which had suffered its first loss the previous week against top-ranked Florida. LSU is one of the toughest places in the country to play. The way the stadium is built, the fans are really close to the field and it can get extremely loud. Plus, it's easy to lose focus since the LSU fans ride you hard when you come back to your sideline after making a mistake. With LSU coming into the game fired up after a loss, we knew we had a difficult assignment ahead of us.

LSU, which had one of the stoutest defenses we would face all season, led 24–0 in the third quarter when we finally got on the board with a field goal by Wes Byrum. Our only touchdown came on the last play of the game to make the final score 31–10.

Although we still had a winning record at 5–3, we had lost three games in a row and had played poorly in each. Things weren't looking good for the Tigers.

HERE WE *DON'T* GO AGAIN

With a three-game losing streak, the first thing I had to do as head coach was assess what we needed to do to stop the bleeding.

As a coaching staff, we had previously established that we wanted to display the same demeanor in front of our players regardless of the outcome of our games. We didn't want the players to see us responding any differently to our recent losses than we had to the earlier wins.

Behind the scenes, though, we reevaluated everything we

had done to that point and reached the conclusion that we had coached during the three-game losing streak the same way we had during the five-game winning streak. So other than a few minor tweaks, we planned to stay the course.

But the most important thing I had to do was evaluate the players. I had to determine if there was an internal problem—if the players were accepting responsibility for the poor play or if they were spreading the blame.

I called in a group of about eight seniors. I started down the line, asking each one, "Why do you think we've lost three games in a row?"

Almost to a man, they answered, "Coach, it's totally our fault. We're not executing. We can see it on the game films. We're sick on Sundays when we watch it. We know what we're doing wrong."

My response to the players was "This is an Auburn problem. This is about us not playing well. But this is fixable. *You* are going to have to fix it."

"Yes, Coach," they replied. "We've got it. We're just getting beat, and we know how to take care of it."

Now that I knew the players were taking responsibility, I had to deliver a message to them. The media was asking questions about our losing streak and bringing up comparisons to the previous season's team, which, like us, had started well—winning four of the first five games—before suffering a four-game losing streak it never recovered from. One reporter asked what lessons this team was learning from last year's team.

My answer went something like this: "There will be no finger-pointing on the team. We all have a choice: do we want to be like we were in the past, or do we want to be different? What I'm saying is that I am proud of our football team, and there is absolutely zero blaming going on, and there won't be. We're going in a new direction right now, and that makes me happy. As long as we execute, we will have a chance to win every game we play. It's that simple."

I wanted to give a vote of confidence to the players who would read my comments. I hoped they would take my statement as a sign of my unwavering expectation that they would snap out of this tailspin. My message to the team was that we didn't care what happened the year before—2009 was not 2008. Nor would it become like 2008.

When the team met on Sunday after the loss, I talked about how there would be no whining. I gave Kodi Burns as an example of how I wanted our players to "man up." Kodi had gotten two teeth knocked out during the game—his teeth literally had to be picked up off the field. He'd also had his lip busted open to the point that he had to have it stitched up during play. But despite the pain and the stitches, Kodi had come back to finish the game. I wanted all our players to have this mind-set of not making any excuses or looking for an easy way out.

"If you wonder why Kodi's an Auburn man, there you go," I told the players. "That's what I want to see. No 'Woe is me.' No 'Your fault.' Man up and go out and play."

11:21

Even though I hadn't detected a "Here we go again" mentality among the players, I knew their confidence needed a boost with a win the following week. We were returning home to face Mississippi, which had a 5–2 record and was ranked twenty-fourth. Ole Miss had been playing well of late, including a 30–17 victory against Arkansas the previous week.

For television purposes, the game was scheduled to start at 11:21 a.m. on Saturday, Halloween morning. That was an earlier start than all but one of our first eight games.

There were a couple of outside forces at work to bolster support for the team leading up to that game.

First, to raise awareness of the kickoff time and to make sure the early start wouldn't affect our fan support, one of our student government leaders started an 11:21 campaign, which included buttons and bumper stickers with a reminder of the start time.

This student had met Jonna the previous weekend at the LSU game. It wasn't the best of introductions, but it turned out to have a surprisingly happy ending.

Jonna was sitting with the other coaches' wives in the stands as usual. As LSU's lead against us climbed, the wives heard increasingly negative comments about our team. The comments also grew more and more personal. One thing Jonna and I have learned over the years is that some fans will turn on a team incredibly fast. It wasn't that long ago that we had been 5–0. What those fans don't realize is how much their negativity affects everyone around them. I promise you it affects the players . . . and in some cases the coaches' families, too.

Coaches' wives are, unfortunately, accustomed to hearing such comments and know it's best to ignore those fans. But for some reason, one particular fan's voice a few rows behind Jonna stood out to her. As he continued to yell rude comments, Jonna stood up, turned to face him, and stared at him.

"What did you say?" she yelled back to him.

He repeated his unflattering comment.

"Oh, that's nice," Jonna said and turned to sit down.

Another coach's wife looked toward the fan. "Do you know who you just spoke to?"

"No," the student replied.

"That's Coach Chizik's wife," she informed him.

A uniformed school police officer who travels with us approached Jonna and the other wives and asked if there was a problem. They filled him in on the situation.

"Are you okay?" he asked Jonna.

"No, I'm not," she answered. She was furious. "If that kid opens his mouth one more time, I'm going to sit next to him and we're going to have a little chat."

The officer asked which fan had been making the comments, and Jonna pointed him out.

The fan stopped his comments at that point, and the situation calmed down. About fifteen or twenty minutes later, though, the student walked down the steps to where Jonna was sitting. He looked directly into her eyes and said, "Mrs. Chizik, I am very sorry. What I said was out of line and unacceptable, and I would like to ask you to forgive me."

Jonna accepted his apology. But we had been emphasizing leadership in talks with our team, and leadership must have been on Jonna's mind because she took advantage of that moment to share publicly with the student some of her thoughts on what it means to be a true leader. "A real leader leads all the time," she told him, "not just when he feels like it." As she was concluding, she told him, "When you're all alone getting ready for bed tonight, I want you to look in the mirror and ask yourself one question: Are you a leader, or are you not? Because right now, from what I've seen, you definitely are not."

He and Jonna eventually wound up having a few positive

conversations. However, I could not have predicted that same student would help lead the 11:21 campaign.

The second scenario that showed something bigger was happening leading up to the Ole Miss game involved a leadership prayer group that Jonna and I belong to. We met with spiritual leaders who prayed with us that God's presence would be evident to many through our football program.

The afternoon before the Ole Miss game, the group prayed at our Jordan-Hare Stadium. We asked God for a miracle to take place inside that stadium—something that the eighty-eight thousand fans in attendance, plus however many people watching on television, would know, beyond a doubt, was a miracle from God. We asked God that his presence there that day would be indisputably recognized.

On the morning of the game, while the players were on the field warming up, wives from the leadership group were together on the sideline. Kristi Malzahn, Gus's wife, received a text from a friend saying that Acts—get this—11:21 had been on her mind that morning. Kristi used her phone to look up the verse.

The wives were stunned when Kristi showed them the verse: "The Lord's hand was with them, and a great number of people believed and turned to the Lord" (NIV).

12

OUR MIRACLE

IT LOOKED LIKE just another one-yard run. We were inside the final three minutes of the first quarter, Ole Miss had the ball near midfield, and we were trailing 7–3. Their running back, Rodney Scott, carried the ball up the middle. Linebacker Josh Bynes filled a hole in the Ole Miss offensive line and wrapped his arms around Scott's ankles as the running back tried to twist out of the tackle.

Safety Zac Etheridge and defensive end Antonio Coleman converged on Scott from opposite sides of the play, and both lowered their shoulders to hit Scott. Scott fell to the ground, and Zac sailed over him. The crown of Zac's helmet hit squarely into Antonio's right shoulder.

Zac landed on Scott. Linebacker Craig Stevens reached down to help Zac off the Ole Miss running back, but Zac didn't move. He remained facedown across Scott's chest.

Running backs are coached to never remain on the ground. They are supposed to immediately get back on their feet and hustle to the huddle for the next play. When a player remains on top of you, your first thought is that your opponent is trying to prevent you from getting back into the game or attempting to start some kind of trouble. So a player who finds himself in a position such as Scott's will almost always push the opposing player off him.

But in this case Rodney Scott didn't do what players typically do. Instead, he lay there on his back, with Zac sprawled on top of him. That probably saved Zac's life.

We could tell Zac was trying to get off Scott. He couldn't. That's when we realized, with growing concern, that he couldn't move at all.

Our medical staff rushed onto the field, and I followed. Zac told our doctors that he couldn't feel anything. Michael Goodlett, our team physician, has since informed me that he feared Zac was permanently paralyzed and might never regain movement.

I got down on both knees and leaned over Zac. Our packed stadium—usually pulsing with cheers and noise—was so quiet that I could hear Scott breathing underneath Zac. Doctors had instructed Scott to remain as still as possible. Dr. Goodlett would tell Zac to wiggle his fingers or his toes. Zac would say he was trying, but he couldn't.

Meanwhile, groups of our players and coaches huddled on the sideline and on the field to pray. Fans were praying in the seats. There were prayers going up for Zac throughout the entire stadium.

For twenty minutes—it seemed agonizingly longer—Zac and Scott remained in their positions.

One couldn't move; the other wouldn't.

A stretcher was called for. The doctors stabilized Zac so they could place him on a backboard. Scott was finally able to get up, and he jogged to join the rest of his teammates at midfield.

It wasn't until after Zac had been placed on the stretcher that he began to regain feeling in his body. Zac told Dr. Goodlett that he would be back on this field playing again. As the stretcher was rolled across the field to an ambulance waiting in the stadium tunnel, Zac raised his right hand to flash a thumbs-up to our fans.

We found out later that Zac was diagnosed with torn neck ligaments and a fractured fifth vertebra. There was also bleeding around the second cervical vertebra, commonly known as the C2. That is where the spinal cord meets the brain. After the game Dr. Goodlett explained to me how potentially serious C2 injuries can be. Not only can C2 trauma cause paralysis, but it can also be fatal.

If Rodney Scott had made a movement under Zac that would have shifted Zac's neck even in the slightest, he could have faced permanent paralysis—or even died. Dr. Goodlett has said he considers it a miracle that Zac wasn't moved in those critical moments.

When the game resumed, it turned into a wild one. We led 10–7 at halftime. But in the third quarter the scoreboard lit up, and both teams collectively racked up thirty-six points. We scored three consecutive touchdowns in only a four-minute span to take a 31–7 lead. After our last touchdown, Ole Miss returned the kickoff for a score. We punted on our next possession, and Ole Miss came right back with another touchdown.

But on the Rebels' extra-point attempt, the snap was fumbled and we blocked the kick. Demond Washington picked up the loose ball and ran it in for a 33–20 Auburn lead. With that swing in our favor, we halted Ole Miss's momentum. The score remained that way through a (thankfully) calm fourth quarter.

On the heels of our three-game losing streak, and having played our worst game of the season the previous week at LSU, this was a significant win for us. It was the best game we'd played all season, and it came at an absolutely critical time. I could sense that our players were feeling pressure to end the losing streak.

After the game in the locker room, though, I said little to the team about the win. Zac's injury was at the forefront of my mind. I talked about how we were going to be playing without a family member for the remainder of the season. This was a time to set football aside and reflect on how easy it is to take life for granted.

"You never know if you're going to have your next play," I reminded the guys. "You never know if you're going to have your next day. You never know if you're going to have your next breath."

Afterward a couple of our players came to me to discuss my postgame comments. "Coach," one of the guys said, "it was really neat what you said to us. What happened to Zac was more important than the win."

I looked at the two of them and said, "Every time. It's just a game."

The day after the Ole Miss game, on Sunday, I called Coach Nutt. "Houston, have you talked to Rodney about what happened?" I asked.

"No, I haven't."

"I've gotta talk to him," I told him. "Can you get me on the phone with him today?"

A short time later I was speaking with Rodney Scott.

I didn't know Rodney. He had committed to Auburn before I took the job, but during the process of changing coaches, he decided to attend Ole Miss instead. We tried to recruit him, but he was firm about going to Ole Miss.

"Rodney, this is Coach Chizik," I said. "First of all, I just want to thank you. I can't even tell you how appreciative I am of you. I don't think you realize how bad it was, buddy, but if you would have moved, that could have been catastrophic."

Then I asked him the two questions I had been wanting to ask. "So tell me, why didn't you move? And how did you know to lie still?"

"Coach," he said, "I can't tell you. It had to be God. Something in my spirit said, 'You lie still. Don't move.'"

"Are you kidding me?" I asked.

"Coach, I can't even explain it. Something inside me told me to stay still."

I was stunned. I couldn't wait to tell our players about my conversation with Rodney.

The story of Zac's injury was big locally. And because of the circumstances surrounding it, it became a national story too. I can't tell you how many hundreds of e-mails our athletic department received from people who were moved by Rodney's account of how he sensed God telling him to remain still. Prayer groups wrote to tell us they were praying for Zac's recovery. The story became a national platform for people to see God at work, and based on the conversations I've had with people about Zac's injury since, I know that the story has made a mighty spiritual impact.

I don't know if, as with the story in Acts 11:21 (NIV), "a great number of people believed and turned to the Lord" because of the miracle that had occurred. But I do know that the Lord's hand was evident that day in our stadium.

FOR NUMBER 4

Zac was released from the hospital two days after the injury and was back at our offices the next day. I had a surprise waiting for him—and one for the rest of the team.

"I have a special guest I want you guys to pay attention to," I told the players in our team meeting room. I didn't reveal the guest's name. "Just make sure you give this speaker your undivided attention when he comes through that door. He's gonna have some good words for you that he wants you to savor."

At that point I opened the door, and Zac and his parents walked in. The players went crazy. They stood and applauded and whooped and hollered.

Zac was wearing a bulky neck brace to keep his head and neck stabilized.

"Zac," I said when the players had settled enough that I could be heard, "we got something for you. We're into November now, and it's getting a little chilly."

He was obviously curious.

"So we got you this." We pulled out an ugly, off-white, extra-large women's turtleneck sweater and tossed it to him.

The whole room erupted again, this time in laughter.

That Saturday we had our final nonconference game, our homecoming game against Furman. We won that one 63–31 after leading 42–3 at halftime. We didn't have Zac in uniform with us, but we did have him with us as part of our uniforms. We felt like we needed to do something special to recognize

Zac, so we got permission from the SEC for our players to wear white wristbands with number 4 on them—Zac's jersey number.

After defeating Furman, we were back in the rankings at number twenty-five and looking to our final two games against conference rivals.

The first was a game at Georgia. The week of that game, senior running back Ben Tate asked if, instead of wearing his usual number 44, he could wear Zac's number 4 to represent him on the field. "No problem," I told Ben. "I like that idea."

Auburn–Georgia is the Deep South's oldest college football rivalry, and this would be the 113th meeting between the schools. To give you an idea how close the competition is, we entered the game with fifty-three wins in the series, Georgia had fifty-one, and there had been eight ties. We had scored 1,698 total points; Georgia had tallied 1,747. Over the span of 112 games, only forty-nine points separated the teams.

It seems like every Auburn–Georgia matchup is a tight, back-and-forth game. This game was no exception.

We scored on our first two possessions to take a 14–0 lead. But our offense slowed from there, and by the end of the third quarter the score was tied at seventeen. Georgia scored early in the fourth quarter to lead by seven points. Demond Washington, however, returned the ensuing kickoff ninety-nine yards for a touchdown, bringing us to another tie, 24–24. With 6:52 left to play, Georgia made a touchdown run to go ahead 31–24.

We answered with a long drive that took us deep into Georgia territory with less than ninety seconds left. I thought we had a tie secured when Chris Todd threw a pass toward the goal line. Mario Fannin was just about to make the catch when Georgia's

Bacarri Rambo came from out of nowhere to hit Mario hard and knock the ball away for an incomplete pass.

Rambo fell to the ground with his right arm extended straight up. The hit had knocked him out. Just two weeks after Zac's injury, we watched as another scary play on the field unfolded. The game was delayed for about ten minutes while Rambo was attended to and carted off the field with what turned out to be a concussion.

Chris was sacked on the next play, and then a five-yard penalty was called against us. On the final play, Chris threw a pass intended for Darvin Adams, but that pass was knocked away too. We lost 31–24.

Auburn's season typically ends with the annual game against rival Alabama in what is known as the Iron Bowl. For many years the game was played at a neutral site in Birmingham, which is an important city in the iron and steel industry. Hence the name.

But the matchup between Auburn and Alabama is more than a rivalry. A team can play against several rivals during a season, but there is one game a year that is personal. For us, Alabama is that opponent.

As we prepared for our season-ending rivalry, I went back and watched the film from the 2008 Auburn–Alabama game. The final score was 36–0, Alabama. I came away with the impression that Auburn's players hadn't taken that game personally enough. It appeared to me that as the game had unfolded, the players had pretty much given up.

We were in a tough spot as we prepared to host Alabama. We were banged up because of injuries, and it had been an up-and-down year for us emotionally. That can drain a team late in the season. Plus, Alabama was undefeated and ranked second in the country. They had their sights set on a national championship.

As I prepared my remarks for the team, I wanted to make it clear to our players that regardless of how the game unfolded or how it would end, it needed to be personal. When you take something personally, you are more intent on doing what needs to be done. That's how humans are wired. I wanted our guys to know that this game was for their pride. This game was for Zac. This game was for Auburn. Anything less than our absolute best was unacceptable.

We didn't have a game the weekend after playing Georgia, so for the entire two weeks leading up to the Alabama game, we talked about making the game personal.

Just as we had against Georgia, we jumped out to a 14–0 lead in the first quarter. On our first possession we scored on an end around when receiver Terrell Zachery took a handoff sixty-seven yards to the end zone. We then called for an onside kick and recovered it.

We had been working on that particular onside kick all season, saving it to pull out for a big game. During our walk-through on Thursday, the day before the game, I gathered the kickoff team. "We will score first in this game and go up by seven," I told them. "And when we get up by seven, we'll come back with this onside kick." I looked at all eleven of them. "Can you execute it?" I asked. "If you can, we'll recover it."

The kickoff team got excited knowing they were finally going to get a chance to deliver the kick they'd been practicing all season. Of course I was kind of painting myself into a corner now that I'd made this announcement to the whole kickoff team.

As part of our take-it-personal exhortations from the previous two weeks, our coaching staff had decided to coach aggressively early in the game. It paid off because we turned that recovered onside kick into another touchdown and a 14–0 lead. Alabama's defense had not allowed a touchdown in its previous two games, but we scored two in the first ten minutes.

But just as in the game against Georgia, we weren't able to hold on to our early lead. Alabama was ranked number two for a reason. They didn't buckle under our early pressure, and by the time the fourth quarter started, we held only a 21–20 lead. The score remained frozen there until Alabama's final possession, when they scored to take their first lead at 26–21.

We got the ball back with 1:24 remaining and drove to Alabama's thirty-seven yard line, but Chris's pass for Kodi Burns on the last play of the game fell incomplete. Alabama beat us 26–21.

I wasn't okay with losing, but I did like our players' mind-set in the two weeks leading up to the game and while we were playing. They had taken to heart what we'd said about making the game personal, and they had played that way against a tough team—a team that, six weeks later, would win the national championship.

"You have laid a foundation for our team," I told our players after the game. "We've been through one year together, and we have set a standard we can live with for a long time here at Auburn. After seeing you out there tonight, I'm convinced we have what we need to move forward and do the things we want to do for Auburn."

Our regular season was over, but because of our 7–5 record, we had earned one more game: a New Year's Day visit to the Outback Bowl.

HAPPY NEW YEAR

It doesn't matter who you're playing—New Year's Day bowl games are special. I can remember watching the parade of bowl games as a kid on New Year's Day. That was the day reserved for the best bowl games played by the best teams. There are more bowl games on that date now than there used to be, but even so, making it into a January 1 game still carries with it an aura of accomplishment.

Our team was off-the-charts ecstatic to be invited to play on New Year's Day. This was a major improvement from the previous season, when they missed playing in a bowl and were home before Christmas.

Our opponent was Northwestern, and we'd be playing in the Outback Bowl in Tampa, Florida. From the moment we received the invitation, we communicated this unwavering message to our players: we were going to Tampa with the sole purpose of returning home with our eighth win. Our school deserved at least eight wins, and it was up to us to deliver.

Northwestern, a member of the Big Ten Conference, had not won a bowl game in sixty-one years, but they were 8–4 and had won their final three games of the regular season, two of which had been against nationally ranked teams.

I knew it was going to be a tough game and it would be hard to pull off a win. I didn't know, however, that we would basically have to win the game four times. We went ahead 35–21 with about seven and a half minutes remaining when senior Ben Tate scored on a seven-yard touchdown run. Ben's touchdown could have pretty much put the game away for us. But after scoring, something told him it would be a good idea to celebrate what was likely the final touchdown of his college career by dunking the football over the crossbar of the goalpost. His dunk drew a fifteen-yard penalty for unsportsmanlike conduct that would be assessed against us on our kickoff.

Ben, a great player who now is in the NFL with the Houston Texans, had really bought into the team-first attitude we had started to cultivate at Auburn. When I met with the players one-on-one in my first days on the job, Ben told me he had contemplated leaving Auburn. I told him I wanted him to stay and play for us, and that if he did, he would notice a lot of favorable changes in our program. But I also said that if he did stay, he was going to have to do whatever we asked of him. He was our star running back, but if we told him we wanted him to play special teams, he'd have to do it. Ben ended up staying and became a 1,400-yard rusher and a warrior for us his senior season.

As Ben came off the field after his dunk, he tried to avoid me. I wouldn't let him get by with that, though. I ripped into him, asking what he was thinking, reminding him that's not what we do at Auburn, and pointing out that his selfishness had cost us a big penalty. Now that the game is more than a year and a half behind us and I'm *mostly* over what Ben did, I can point out that it wasn't even a very good dunk. We can finally joke about it now.

Because of the penalty on the kickoff, Northwestern had good field position to start its next drive, and they marched downfield for a touchdown. We blocked the extra-point kick to keep our lead at eight points, 35–27.

Northwestern attempted an onside kick that we recovered, and we had a chance to run out the clock, but Ben fumbled on our second play and Northwestern recovered. That led to another touchdown for the Wildcats with 1:15 remaining. Northwestern needed a two-point conversion to tie the score, and they got it on a trick play.

We returned the ensuing kickoff to midfield but fumbled at the end of the return and gave the ball right back to Northwestern. Their forty-four-yard field goal attempt on the final play of regulation sailed just wide of the uprights, and we dodged that bullet to go into overtime.

We had the ball first in overtime, and Wes Byrum made a twenty-one-yard field goal to give us a 38–35 lead. Northwestern got the ball with a chance to either match our field goal and force a second overtime or score a touchdown to win the game.

On Northwestern's fourth play we hit the quarterback and caused a fumble that we recovered. We ran onto the field to celebrate our victory. But the play was reviewed by the replay official, who determined that the quarterback was down before losing the ball. Northwestern retained possession.

Our defense forced Northwestern into a fourth down situation and a thirty-seven-yard field goal attempt that could have tied the score. The kick was missed. Again we started onto the field to celebrate. But there was a flag on the ground. We had roughed the kicker, and that penalty gave Northwestern a first down at our nine yard line. Our defense held once more. On fourth down at our five, Northwestern sent its field goal unit back into the game. But this time the backup kicker came jogging onto the field. The starting kicker had been hurt on our earlier penalty.

With the backup kicker in, we coaches had our eyes open for some kind of trick play. When we saw Northwestern line up in a kick formation that was different from their previous one, we started yelling for our players to watch for a fake field goal. I don't think the players heard us, but they still made a game-saving play.

Northwestern did run a trick play, getting the ball in the hands of a receiver on an old fumblerooski-type play. Our Neiko Thorpe sniffed out the trick, though, and pushed the ballcarrier out of bounds two yards short of the goal line.

We ran onto the field to celebrate again—but this time it was legitimate. We really had won our eighth game.

We were all excited on the field, as you can imagine, and Ben Tate came up to me. I don't even remember hearing what he said. "I'm not talking to you right now," I joked with him. "I'm too mad at you."

Ben left school after the bowl game to prepare for the NFL draft. The night after National Signing Day in February, he left me a voice mail.

"Coach," he said, "I just wanted to call you and congratulate you on your signing class. That's awesome. And I also want to apologize for dunking the ball over that goalpost. I'll be around soon, and I'll be by to see you guys."

I clicked off the message and thought about how far Ben had come from that day he told me he was considering leaving Auburn. He trusted the changes we were making and he became an example of a guy with a team-over-me attitude.

The Ben Tate on that message was not the same person of a year earlier. When you get a message like that, you know that you are making an impact. That's how I receive my validation as a coach.

GOOD TO GREAT

Winning eight games in my first year was important for our program. So was the way we won that eighth game.

I believe that our players, after having failed to make a bowl game the previous season, would have been happy just to be in a New Year's Day game. But we wouldn't let them settle for that. We pushed them to win—not just for themselves, but for the future of the program.

After watching our players fight for the win, I knew they understood what it took to be champions. There were three moments when we thought we had won. Each of those moments instead turned out to be circumstances that could have caused us to get discouraged and let the game slip through our fingertips. But we ignored the impostors. We battled through the shifting emotions, and we won.

Our players had shown that they understood the importance of fighting for Auburn and that the Auburn family we talked about was real. They realized we were a legitimate program—the place they wanted to spend the rest of their college careers.

And that's when I felt it for the first time: we had achieved the complete trust I'd promised the players in our very first meeting.

On the flight home, I reviewed our season. I felt like we had laid a foundation we could build on. We'd had a good season. But I thought, *I don't just want to be good. I've been on great football teams, and I miss it. I want Auburn football to be great.*

I needed to determine what we had to do to move from good to great.

A week after the bowl game, I made that our team's mantra: *Good to great.* Good was no longer enough. We were working to be great.

13

ALL IN

ONE DAY BEFORE we played in the Outback Bowl, we made an addition to our team that would prove to be a key component in our transformation from good to great. His name was Cameron Newton, and he was an athletic freak of nature.

Cameron was a six-foot-six, 250-pound quarterback at Blinn College, a junior college in Texas. For comparison's sake, Chris Todd was six foot two, 210 pounds, and Chris was a good-size quarterback in his own right.

I, however, wasn't interested in bringing in a junior college quarterback. I prefer longevity at the quarterback position, and when you take on a junior college quarterback, you have to develop him quickly. You have him for only two years, and then you have to replace him already. When you recruit a quarterback straight from high school, you'll have him in your program for four years, and he brings more of a stabilizing factor to the team.

Curtis Luper, our running backs coach, had visited Blinn to take a look at a receiver, but he came back raving about the quarterback he'd seen there.

"Yeah, Curtis, that's good," I said. "We're not taking a junior college quarterback."

"No, Coach," Curtis said. "I think you really need to take a look at him."

The conversation fizzled there.

A few days later Curtis brought up the quarterback from Blinn again. I repeated my earlier stance: thanks, but no thanks.

Still, the offensive staff wouldn't let this one go, and I finally relented. We agreed that Cameron could come in before Christmas for an official recruiting visit.

I remember my initial reaction when Cameron walked through my office door. I looked at him and thought, *Wow, that's the best-looking defensive end I've ever seen.*

Except that Cameron was a quarterback.

I don't want a junior college quarterback, I told myself, *so I'm not spending a lot of time with him. I know that the more time I spend with him, the more I'm going to want to keep him.*

Cameron spent a weekend visiting us, and I absolutely fell in love with his personality. He had a big, bright smile, and there was a quality about him that seemed to communicate Auburn potential.

After Cameron left, I called in the players who had spent the most time with him during his visit. Each of those players loved him too. They said he was fairly quiet and just sat back and blended in with the players. In their opinion, he would be a good fit for our program.

We offered Cameron a scholarship and waited to see if he

would accept. While we were in Tampa preparing for the Outback Bowl, Cameron told us he would accept our offer. We were elated. But at that point we didn't see him as the Cameron Newton most fans are familiar with now.

I wasn't sure how much of a chance he had of becoming our starting quarterback. For one thing, he was coming from a junior college, and there are always questions about the quality of competition there. Until you can get a player on the field with other guys at our level, you're not really sure what you have to work with. Plus, Cameron had initially attended Florida before transferring to Blinn, and I wondered how good he could be if he had left Florida for a junior college. One thing I was sure about was that we had nobody else on our team with his athletic ability. Still, the quarterback position is about so much more than ability.

As we looked into Cameron's history, we discovered that he had left Florida under some controversy. Before we offered Cameron a scholarship, we checked into the issues at Florida. We asked Cameron about what had happened, and we were satisfied with the answer he gave us. I also checked with a coach who had been at Florida at the time, asking him this question: "Putting football aside—from a character standpoint alone—if you were the head coach at Auburn, would you want him in your program?" His answer was an emphatic yes.

Then I talked with Brad Franchione, Cameron's coach at Blinn. He told me that Cam was, beyond the shadow of a doubt, a great kid and that we should take him. When I asked Coach Franchione if his team would have won their championship without Cameron, he said no. He told me that Cameron had been great with his children and that he and his wife loved Cam's personality. Coach Franchione was 100 percent supportive of our offering Cameron a scholarship.

Based on the digging we had done, I was comfortable bringing Cameron to Auburn.

After getting back from the Outback Bowl and before Cameron would report to school for the spring semester, I visited Cameron and his family in his home. Something happened there that has never happened in all my years of recruiting. When I stood up to leave, Cameron asked if we could pray together. We all held hands in his living room, and Cameron led us in prayer. That boldness for his faith really caught my attention.

When Cameron came to campus to start the semester, I explained that we didn't have a starting quarterback yet but that he would not have the starter position handed to him. If the spot were to become his, he would have to earn it. He said he wouldn't want it any other way.

Within the first couple of weeks of spring practices, it was obvious that starting Cameron would give us the best chance to win and that the team was ready for him to step into that position. He had learned our offense, and we could see he was continuously getting better at running it. On top of that, his confidence was growing. There were no gimmes for Cam—we were tough on him. I don't know how many bear crawls Coach Malzahn had him do for any little thing he did wrong on the field. But he handled every bit of pressure we put on him just the way a leader should.

Even so, we didn't name him the starter then. We kept the starting position open all spring to give everyone a fair chance. We also knew, though, that we didn't want to have the quarterback situation go unresolved into the summer like we'd had to do with Chris Todd and Kodi Burns our first off-season. There's something innate that makes players want to know who their leader will be. Also, with summer workouts being strictly voluntary due to NCAA regulations, a team needs a leader who will take charge during the summer. If a coaching staff is ready to name its starting quarterback before summer hits, it's the best scenario for the team. And we were ready.

Right when spring ball ended, we brought each of the quarterback candidates in and told them who the starter would be.

When I informed Cameron the position was his, he said, "I can't believe it." In fact, I think he even said that multiple times.

I then launched into my starting quarterback speech. "You've earned it. You've done everything we've asked you to do, and you deserve it. Make sure you know that you're the starter right now and that your job is to do everything you can to continue to be the starter. Because if you don't, you won't be the starter. This is not a license for you to coast because you've won the job. This is an opportunity for you to press on with even more urgency than you have before. You are the leader of this football team. This summer you're the one who's going to lead this team. And if you're not doing it the way we want you to do it, I can very easily go to the next guy. And I will."

I also wanted to give Cameron an introduction to the pressure he would face as Auburn's starting quarterback.

"Other than the governor of Alabama," I told him, "the four most recognizable people in this state are me, you, Nick Saban, and Alabama's starting quarterback. There are more than four and a half million people in this state, and everything you do, everything you say, everywhere you go, you need to understand what sword you're carrying here. And you're carrying it for a bunch of folks now. So this is a big job—and it's not just about throwing a football. I need you to grasp the enormity of this."

"Yes, sir," he said. "I've got it."

Before Cameron left my office, he had one more thing he wanted to say.

"Coach, all I can tell you is that you will not regret this. I want you to know my goal is not just to win. I want to win it *all*. I want to win the national championship."

SETTING EXPECTATIONS

I didn't put any kind of expectations on the team in terms of victory totals as we headed into preseason. Instead, my main goal was to put a team on the field that understood how to compete. I wanted a team that would show up week in and week out, doing what it took to become champions.

Almost every day Trooper Taylor, our assistant head coach and a great motivator, would ask the players, "What did you come to Auburn to win?"

"Championships!" the players would answer each time.

Trooper had started asking this question before the 2009 season, but I'm not convinced the players truly believed their answer that year. Going into 2010, I thought our players believed we had a chance to win a lot of games, but I wasn't sure they had the faith that we could really win a championship.

Each day we talked to the players about being the best at their trade. Like blacksmiths or welders who seek to fine-tune their craft, our players needed to be at the top of their game if they wanted to have a chance to become champions.

They needed to compete. That was it.

I didn't set a magic number for victories. We were going to

start with the goal of winning championships; then on a daily basis, each player would work to become the best at his trade. The players could make the team better by making themselves better. If every player did that, we'd be ready to do what we'd come to Auburn to do: win championships.

TURNING UP THE HEAT

In mid-August, less than two weeks before our season opener, I thought Cameron needed a little shake-up.

We had started preseason practices the first week of August; then we moved into two-a-days. Cameron, along with the rest of the team, had grown tired during two-a-days. That's part of the typical practice flow when you're preparing for the upcoming season. But I had a lingering question about Cameron as our starting quarterback.

I knew he was athletic. He was looking even more comfortable running our offense, and his passing was improving. Those were all things I could monitor in practice. But there was a question that practices could not answer: could he handle the pressure?

I called Cameron in to meet with Coach Malzahn and me. I wanted to put some heat on Cam now to see how he would respond.

"Listen," I said, looking directly at Cameron. My tone was pretty firm. "I don't know if you're ready for this. I really don't. You're gonna have to show me something in practice right now that makes me think you're ready to be our starter. You need to do more than you're doing now. You have not convinced me that if you throw three interceptions and we lose and the media is all over you, you're the guy who can handle it."

Then I looked at Gus. "Gus, really and truly, we need to look at starting another guy. He ain't ready. He ain't focused. I don't think he can handle the pressure of the SEC."

Cameron nodded. "Coach, I understand. I'll get it done." He took what I said personally, but he also took it like a man. Then he went out there and proved me wrong. I'm glad he did.

In practices, Cameron never complained about the heat we were putting on him. He never whined. He passed all the tests we threw at him, but I still wanted to see how he would handle a game day situation.

We opened the season at home against Arkansas State the first Saturday in September. We didn't know how good Arkansas State would be. And there was something else we didn't know before taking the field: how difficult Cameron would be to tackle.

We can't afford to have our starting quarterback get injured in practice, so we tend to be extra protective of these guys. Whenever Cameron would run with the ball in practice, we'd blow the whistle to end the play anytime a defender got near him. In our preseason talks, Gus and I had decided to limit Cameron to about seven or eight called running plays per game. We knew there would be times he would drop back to pass and wind up running the ball out of the pocket, and we figured that including those times, Cameron would have fewer than a dozen carries per game. We wanted to prevent him from taking too much of a beating during games.

That's not quite how things panned out our first game. Cameron had fifteen carries against Arkansas State and rushed for 171 yards and two touchdowns. His second touchdown came late in the second quarter on a seventy-one-yard run on which no defender even came close to putting a hand on him. The crowd roared their approval. I looked at Gus, and he just kind of shrugged his shoulders. Cameron was so big and physical that he was a beast for Arkansas State to tackle. And by the way, he also was nine for fourteen passing, racking up 186 yards and three touchdowns.

That game also marked Zac Etheridge's miraculous return from injury. It was an emotional day for Zac, especially after the nine-month journey he had taken to put on his Auburn uniform again.

Zac's mother, Cassandra Kelly, is a God-fearing woman, and she kept telling me, "If the good Lord wants my son to play again, he'll play."

In my mind, I was thinking, *There's no way he can come back from an injury like that.* In my conversations with Jonna, I told her, "If that were my son, his career would be over. I wouldn't care if the doctors told him he could come back or not. I wouldn't do it."

But Zac and his parents truly believed that God would clear a path for him to return safely. Sure enough, he came back.

When doctors gave permission for Zac to resume football activities without contact, we requested and received a waiver from the NCAA that would allow him to work out while wearing a helmet during the summer. NCAA rules ban players from wearing helmets during summer workouts, but we needed to see if Zac could carry the weight before he was in a game situation. The next step was to add shoulder pads and see how Zac's body would handle that.

Right before two-a-days began in August, Zac flew to Dallas to meet with a highly respected surgeon who works with the Dallas Cowboys. We didn't see any outward signs that anything was wrong with Zac's neck, but Dr. Goodlett and our medical staff wanted to take extra precautions to ensure Zac wasn't endangering himself. Zac's mom always told me that she knew God had a plan for her son's life and that she believed his returning to the field was part of that plan.

I love a mother's faith.

The Dallas doctor studied a series of MRIs on Zac's neck and was astonished at the healing that had taken place over the past few months. He said that if he'd looked at the first MRI compared with the last one without any background, he never would have guessed they were of the same person. When a doctor says a miracle has occurred, you know where the ultimate healing has come from.

Fully assured that Zac was at no greater risk of injury than anyone else on the field, we eased him back into our practices and preseason scrimmages to prepare him for the season opener.

It was a momentous Tiger Walk for Zac the day of the Arkansas State game. He stopped when he saw his parents in the front row along the route, embraced them, and gave his ever-faithful mom a kiss on the cheek.

On the field during pregame warm-ups, I walked over to Zac and shook his hand, then embraced him with my other arm.

"God bless you, bro," I said to him. "It's going to be a good day."

"It's gonna be a great one, Coach," he replied.

And indeed it was. We won 52–26.

LEANING ON EACH OTHER

We had a quick turnaround leading up to our next game, a Thursday night conference matchup at Mississippi State that was being broadcast on ESPN. We won 17–14 in a tough defensive battle. Mississippi State had a strong team that year (they wound up winning nine games, including a bowl game against Michigan), but we were ready for them.

Cameron ran for seventy yards on eighteen carries and threw both of our touchdown passes. Michael Dyer, a freshman running back, played a significant role for us in that game. We knew he had the talent, but the unknown with freshman running backs is always whether they will be prone to fumble, especially in pressure situations.

We were ahead 17–14 midway through the fourth quarter, and we entrusted the ball to Michael. We ran seven plays on one possession, and five were handoffs to Michael. He protected the ball and moved us into field goal range. Our kick was blocked, though, and Mississippi State took over on its twenty yard line with two minutes left.

Our defense was going to have to win this game—or at least prevent Mississippi State from sending the game into overtime. Mississippi State drove to our forty-one, but our defense forced four consecutive incomplete passes to land us the win. With all the national attention, and with the added hype of a televised game, that was a pivotal victory for us. Beating the Bulldogs gave us confidence that we could go on the road and win a physical SEC game against a good team. Circumstances weren't always the best for us during that game, but I saw the beginnings of a team that was being molded into championship material.

That also was the game when our team started a new tradition: singing "Lean on Me" as part of our weekly postgame routine in the locker room. It all began at the team devotional the night before, when the guys in the hotel meeting room sang the song at the beginning of devotions. After we defeated Mississippi

State, the players decided to put their arms around each other and sing the song together. The coaches joined in too.

I wasn't too worried about anyone from the Auburn music department trying to recruit my players to join a choir, but it was a bonding moment for all of us. The song was appropriate, too, because the way that particular game had played out, we all—the offense, the defense, the special teams, and the coaches—had leaned on each other to win.

Each week ESPN selects one game from which to anchor its all-day Saturday menu of football games. The network sends its *College GameDay* crew of announcers to the site of the game with a full broadcast set and invites fans to come out and create a frenzy of activity behind the show hosts. ESPN sent its hosts and crew to Auburn for our third game, a home game against Clemson. Both teams were 2–0, and we had cracked the top twenty in the national rankings for the first time—number sixteen in the media poll and number fifteen in the coaches' poll.

Jeff Grimes, our offensive line coach, had recently used the phrase "all in" when talking to our offense about Colossians 3:23, which reads, "Work willingly at whatever you do, as though you were working for the Lord rather than for people." Jeff shared that when he was coaching at a school that didn't have as much talent as other teams, they had still been successful because the players had been "all in."

All in.

Those words resonated with Tim Jackson, our executive associate athletics director, who had been sitting in on that meeting. A few days later Tim came to me and sold me on a marketing strategy that would make "all in" a key phrase not only for coaches and players but also for our students and fans. Having everybody all in seemed to be the answer to my post–Outback Bowl question of what we needed to do to move beyond good and into the realm of great. Jeff might not have realized it at the time, but his remark gave our team a motto that would come to define our 2010 season.

With ESPN coming to set up shop outside Jordan-Hare Stadium, we wanted to build the hype for Saturday's game and decided to hold an on-campus pep rally Wednesday night. We didn't have much time to plan, and we ended up sending an e-mail to students just one day before the rally. Because of the short notice, we didn't know how many students would show up. Maybe a few hundred, we hoped.

We were stunned when we got to the pep rally on Wednesday—there were people everywhere. I spoke to the students for about five minutes. They belonged to the Auburn family, and I wanted them to understand the role they could play in preparing us for the Clemson game. "I just got done with practice, and the speech I gave our football team was simply this: It's Wednesday night. I don't need 'em ready to play tonight. I need 'em ready to play Saturday night. But here's what I need right now. I need every guy on that team all in. I need everybody on that field all in. And here's my message to you: I need each one of you all in on Saturday. I need you all in at eight o'clock in the morning with *GameDay*. I need you all in at kickoff. I need you all in at halftime."

The students went nuts cheering when I finished. Tim had helped get one thousand T-shirts printed with the school's *AU* logo on them. *FAMILY* was printed underneath the logo, and beneath that in bigger letters it read, *ALL IN*. I heard they had expected to hand out about two hundred to three hundred shirts that night, but with the size of the crowd, all one thousand were gone in a matter of minutes.

The excitement from the pep rally carried all the way to early Saturday morning, when ESPN went live from our campus. Our fans did a great job showing up and making noise for the cameras. The atmosphere on campus was even more festive than usual for a game day. It was a good thing, too, because as it turned out, we needed all the support we could get.

Remember when I first came to Auburn and asked players whether they thought we could come back and win if we fell behind by two touchdowns? And remember how they weren't sure we could?

Well, we fell behind Clemson 17–0 in the second quarter. Nothing was going our way until late in the first half when we put together a drive that allowed Wes Byrum to kick a field goal on the final play before halftime. Still, even when we were trailing by such a deficit, our team never flinched. The players' demeanor gave no indication that we were getting outplayed by a significant margin.

We came out in the third quarter and scored three consecutive touchdowns to take a 24–17 lead. Clemson tied the score early in the fourth quarter, but regulation play ended without either offense having another serious scoring opportunity.

We had the ball first in overtime, and Wes kicked a thirty-nine-yard field goal to give us a 27–24 lead. When Clemson had possession, they reached our eight yard line before our defense halted their drive. They made a twenty-six-yard field goal that appeared to send the game to a second overtime, but Clemson was flagged for an illegal procedure on the kick. Backed up five yards due to the penalty, Clemson missed the next field goal attempt.

Despite trailing 17–0, we had come back to win 27–24.

BETTER LATE THAN NEVER

The week of our fourth game, against South Carolina, I noted in practice that Cameron was starting to look like a quarterback who could play in the NFL. I had coached teams with future NFL quarterbacks in the past, such as Daunte Culpepper, Jason Campbell, Vince Young, and Colt McCoy, and Cameron was starting to get the same pro-potential look to him I had seen in those other athletes. His passing had improved, and he was now zipping passes into narrow openings to receivers. His confidence was growing too.

That week Gus and I decided to forget any ideas of trying to limit Cam's carries. He had proved that with his size and agility, he could handle the defensive pressure.

"He's a horse," I told Gus. "We're going to start giving him the ball twenty-five times a game. What do you think?"

Gus was all for it.

"I'm with you," he said. "Let's do it."

Cameron had exactly twenty-five carries against South Carolina for a total of 176 yards and three touchdowns. We'd had to come from behind again—this time from a thirteen-point deficit in the second quarter.

Cameron ran for touchdowns in the second and third quarters to help us take a 21–20 lead. South Carolina went up 27–21 in the third quarter. But Cameron threw two touchdowns in the fourth quarter, and the defense came through with two interceptions to seal the 35–27 victory, bringing our overall record to 4–0.

We hosted Louisiana-Monroe the following week and won that game with no problem, 52–3, setting us up for a game the next Saturday at Kentucky. This was our second road game of the season and the first for which we would be flying. We had our short walk-through Friday, and when I dismissed the players, I told them the bus was leaving for the airport in twenty-five minutes and reminded everyone to make sure they had their IDs so they could board the plane.

I was getting ready to head down from my office to the bus when I received a phone call from Trooper Taylor. It was three minutes past the time we had told players to be on the bus, and he asked me if the team could have a couple more minutes because not everyone was aboard.

"No," I said. "Who's not there?"

"Cameron Newton," he said.

"Where is he?"

"Well, he didn't have his ID on him, so we sent him over to campus to get an ID made."

"Well, we're leaving," I said.

"No, no, let's just wait. He's almost back. He's right around the corner."

"No, we're leaving. Load up the bus. I don't care who it is— we're leaving."

So I made my way to the bus, and off we went to the air-port . . . without Cameron. Tim Jackson, who was traveling with us, had made arrangements for Cameron to get a ride to the airport—unbeknownst to Cam, of course.

I want to tell you that Cameron had never been late for any-thing before. In fact, he had been on time for the bus that day. He just didn't have his ID and thought he could get one made on campus faster than he could go home to retrieve his and get back to the bus.

Meanwhile, everyone on the bus was freaking out. The offensive linemen were freaking out because they knew that look on my face. Coach Malzahn was freaking out at the thought of his quarterback not playing against Kentucky because he had missed the bus. Everybody was panicking but me. There was a means to this madness.

First, I knew that Cameron was on his way to being an extremely special player. But I didn't want him to think he was going to be treated any differently on our team. Second, I thought he needed to be more focused for the game. In my opinion, he had looked too loose at the walk-through and he needed to be redirected. I also thought this would be a great time for his teammates to come to his rescue. And they did, by asking Tim if he could talk to me about backing off on Cameron a little bit. The entire offensive line went to Tim to see if I would let Cameron play.

Cameron's ride had him at the airport only ten minutes after the team bus had arrived, but I asked that he be kept in the car so I could talk to him. He got a pretty good blistering.

"You're not focused right now," I said. "You're lucky we're still here. Personally I don't care if you have to walk to Lexington. We're going to play football with or without you. You could have been left behind." Actually, the situation wasn't that much of an issue to me, but I thought it would be a good opportunity to remind him that one person is not bigger than the team.

Cameron was quiet on the plane and the rest of Friday night. The next day, about an hour before we left for the stadium, I had a little talk with him.

"Cam, you know I love you. You know what? I laid into you because I don't think you're ready to play. I don't think you're focused."

"Coach," he told me, "I needed that. You're right, and everything you did was right on."

"I trust you," I said. "And I love you. I can't wait to watch you play tonight because you are going to have a fantastic game."

And he did. He absolutely took over the game. He rushed for 198 yards on twenty-eight carries with four touchdowns. He also passed for 210 yards and led our offense on a nineteen-play, game-ending drive that concluded with Wes's twenty-four-yard field goal with no time on the clock for a 37–34 victory. Cameron showed just how special a player he was in that game.

WE CAN WIN IT ALL

After Cameron's impressive showing at Kentucky, his name was beginning to pop up in conversations about potential Heisman Trophy winners. Our team was getting some buzz too. With our 6–0 record, we had moved up to seventh in both rankings. Next up was Arkansas, which was coming into Jordan-Hare Stadium ranked twelfth with a 4–1 record.

The Arkansas game was a shootout, setting a record for the most combined points ever scored in an SEC game that didn't go into overtime. I'm a defensive-minded coach, so high-scoring games like that can be a little tough on me, but as long as we're doing more scoring than our opponent, I'm good.

We were losing 43–37 after Arkansas scored a touchdown with 14:09 left in the fourth quarter. The way we had moved the ball up to that point, there wasn't much doubt we would score some more. What would determine whether we would win was if our defense could find a way to slow down Arkansas's high-powered offense.

We took the lead back barely two minutes after the Arkansas touchdown when Cameron hit Emory Blake for a touchdown pass. The Razorbacks' reserve quarterback, Tyler Wilson, was in the game because starter Ryan Mallett had been hit in the head in the first half. But Wilson played like a starter against us, throwing four touchdown passes after entering the game.

In the end, though, our defense came through for us. After we regained the lead, our defense held Arkansas scoreless the rest of the way. Zac Etheridge scored our next touchdown on a fumble return. Cameron had a short touchdown run soon after, and Michael Dyer had a thirty-eight-yard touchdown run midway through the fourth quarter, giving us a 65–43 victory.

We had found another way to win. This time it was simply by outscoring the other team.

The next day in our coaches meeting, I walked in, looked at everybody, and said, "Guys, we can win it all."

You won't find me that far out on a limb very often.

But this season was different. I firmly believed we had a chance to go undefeated the rest of the way and win the national championship. When I said that to our coaches, I think every one of them nodded in agreement. I realized I wasn't the only one thinking that way. It wasn't just because of how well Cameron was playing—and he certainly had been playing well and bringing leadership to the locker room and offensive huddle. But our entire team was gaining confidence.

It's good for a team to have confidence, of course, but that can also make us coaches a little cautious. The last thing we want to do in a situation like that is to become overconfident. The first BCS rankings of the season had come out the day after the Arkansas game, and we were ranked fourth. Since only the top two teams at the end of the regular season would play for the national championship, we couldn't afford to overlook a single game, as even one loss would cause us to slide down in the rankings.

I didn't talk to the players about our national title chances. Instead, I went back to our "Good to great" mantra.

"Guys, you don't know what great looks like yet," I cautioned. "But if you keep going in the direction you're headed, and if you compete at a level that's beyond anything you've done before, you will get there. And when you eventually arrive, there will be no doubt in your minds. You will know what great looks like.

"Don't take any steps backward," I concluded. "We're not at the level of great yet. But I'm confident that we have the talent and the heart to get there. If we keep moving forward, if we stay all in, we will experience *great*."

14

NO DISTRACTIONS

WITH OUR NEXT GAME, our eighth of the season, we would say good-bye to normalcy around our program.

We knew it would be a big game. LSU came to Jordan-Hare Stadium for a matchup of the last two unbeaten teams in the conference. LSU was ranked just behind us in the BCS rankings, at number six. The general opinion was that we had the SEC's best offense and LSU had the conference's best defense.

Anticipation for the game was so high that our school issued a warning to fans about the potential of people selling counterfeit tickets. And the game lived up to the hype.

The score was 10–10 in the third quarter when Cameron broke into what we still refer to around here as "The Run"—a forty-nine-yard touchdown run that displayed his rare combination of strength and speed. He ran straight up the middle and powered through two would-be tacklers. The second defender caused him to stumble briefly, but he stayed on his feet. When he broke out into the open field, twice he made cuts that left defenders diving to attempt arm tackles. Then, at about the twenty yard line, he accelerated and dragged the final defender five yards into the end zone.

We were tied 17–17 early in the fourth quarter, and although we had never been behind, we also had not led by more than seven points. It was a physical, hard-fought game between two excellent teams. With 5:05 to play, we scored the go-ahead touchdown when Onterio McCalebb, who had carried the ball only three times in the game, took a handoff on a sweep around the left end and raced seventy yards to the end zone.

We held LSU without a first down on the next possession. After taking over when we stopped LSU on fourth down, we kept Cameron rushing and ran the ball all the way to the LSU five before taking a knee on the final play for a 24–17 win.

After that game I could tell our players had begun to believe they could win the national championship. Beating a championship-caliber team like that proved to our guys that they really had what it takes to win.

The hype over our game also intensified the hoopla about Cameron's performance. He had carried the ball twenty-eight times for 217 yards and two touchdowns, crossing the 1,000-yard mark for the season and breaking the SEC record for rushing yards in a season by a quarterback. The old record had been set by another Auburn quarterback, Jimmy Sidle, in 1963.

After the LSU game and "The Run," Cameron became the front-runner for the Heisman, and the national media attention around him reached fever pitch. I called him into my office on

Sunday. I don't like talking to players about personal achievements, and Cameron wasn't the type who walked around bragging about his own accomplishments. He preferred to blend in with the rest of the players, but that was becoming difficult now that he was being singled out by the Heisman hype. I had put off having this talk for two weeks, but it was time. I asked Cameron's parents, still in town from the previous day's game, to sit down with us.

"You're on track right now for the Heisman," I told him. "Unless there is a complete change from this point, you've got a great chance to win it. Do you remember that first day we named you starting quarterback and I told you that, not counting the governor, you would be one of the four most recognizable people in Alabama? Well, now there's no doubt about it. You are the most recognized guy in this state. And you're slowly but surely becoming the most recognized player in college football.

"Make sure you understand that as your world grows on the outside, and as this media attention becomes an even bigger monster, your personal world needs to shrink. Everybody is going to want a piece of you. I'm saying this to watch out for you: your world has to become smaller than it is now. This is *imperative* if you're going to protect yourself."

I could see where everything was headed. I felt like I needed to warn Cameron that the remainder of the season would not get any easier for him. It was only going to become more intense as we continued to win games and as he continued to perform at a Heisman level. Cameron got it. He understood what I was saying.

With the media attention and demands growing, we needed to protect Cameron to the best of our ability. If we didn't help with his daily schedule, the demands would become impossible to manage. Tim Jackson came to me with a detailed plan to take over Cam's schedule, monitor his appointments, and manage his media requests. Tim was the perfect person for the job. He's the number two person to athletic director Jay Jacobs and another true Auburn man, having worked in the school's athletic department for more than two decades.

I had met Tim at a coaching convention back when I was a graduate assistant at Clemson, and I got to know him well when I was defensive coordinator at Auburn. Tim brings a beneficial and unique dynamic to our team. He serves as a bridge because he is an administrator who is also attached to the football side of our operation. He's on the field with us, he's in every staff meeting, and he's with us on our trips. His presence prevents what in many universities becomes a gap between football and the administration. He understands both sides and keeps us working together toward the same purpose. Tim is my right-hand man, and we work closely together on a daily basis.

The players know Tim has my ear, and he's someone they can go to at any time with any issue. If for whatever reason they are not comfortable bringing up a concern with me or another coach, they can go to Tim and know that I will listen to what he has to say.

In the midst of the building craziness for Cameron, Tim was able to help keep everything under control. Cameron probably felt like he had a bodyguard at times because Tim would protect him and act as a buffer between him and all the people who wanted a piece of him. Otherwise there would have been times when Cameron didn't even make it to class. Cameron is a people pleaser, and many times Tim had to step in and say no on his behalf. Tim had a difficult role that required making some people unhappy, but without him, Cameron's situation would have become overwhelming. To this day, Tim is probably closer with Cameron than anyone else at Auburn because of the trust and the relationship they developed during that time.

OUR MIRACLE REVISITED

The LSU win vaulted us to number one in the BCS rankings for the first time since the rankings began in 1998. If we stayed within the top two spots, we would be in position to play for the national championship. Meanwhile, Cameron was being touted nationwide as the Heisman favorite.

On top of that, we were going to Oxford, Mississippi, to face Ole Miss for the first time since Zac Etheridge's injury. The stories about Zac and his upcoming reunion with Ole Miss's Rodney Scott put back into the spotlight the miracle God had worked on our field a year earlier.

There was a lot going on surrounding that game, but as was characteristic of our players all season, they kept their focus on football and we took care of business. We won, but we had to do it in a different manner than we had in the past.

Ole Miss's defense was determined not to let Cameron beat them. Cameron had relatively low numbers in the game, rushing eleven times for forty-five yards. He was able to throw for 209 yards and two touchdowns, but the defense's focus on stopping him created openings for other players. Michael Dyer, our freshman running back, rushed for 180 yards and a touchdown, and Onterio McCalebb had another long touchdown run—sixty-eight yards this time—as part of his ninety-nine rushing yards.

Ole Miss is another difficult place to play in the SEC, but we scored ten points in the last two and a half minutes of the first half to lead 34–17 as we went into the locker room. Our lead had grown to 44–17 by the end of the third quarter, and we enjoyed a sizable lead throughout the fourth quarter. We ended up winning by the comfortable margin of 51–31.

After the game I was able to thank Rodney in person for what he had done for Zac. It was the first time Zac and Rodney had spoken face-to-face since the injury. They had talked by phone in the first few days after Zac was released from the hospital, and they had called each other a couple of times per month since.

They were unable to meet up before the game, and Rodney didn't play that day, so the two of them weren't on the field at the same time. But afterward Zac and his family connected with Rodney. When players from both teams met at midfield for a postgame prayer, Zac, his family, and Rodney joined in and prayed together.

Although we played really well against Ole Miss, the real adventure turned out to be off the field after the game.

During the off-season after our schedule had been set, Tim came to talk with me about travel arrangements for the Ole Miss game. We could either take four buses to Oxford, about a three-hundred-mile trip, or fly to Memphis and then bus about eighty miles to Oxford.

Tim suggested we go the bus route because flying would save us only about thirty minutes and we would have to deal with the hassles of flying and transferring from the plane to buses. Plus, he thought the uninterrupted time on the buses could serve a team bonding function. "It'll be good for our players," he said. He talked me into busing the whole way.

The trip home did turn into a time of bonding—but not in the way we might have expected.

What was supposed to be a five-hour trip turned into a six-hour trip. We made a stop on the way home because the bus drivers were required to take a short break after a certain amount of time on the road. During the stop a few players asked if they could go inside the rest area to use the facilities. A few turned into ten, and then some other guys wanted to go in to get candy bars. And then some more wanted to go in to buy drinks. I don't remember all the reasons the players came up with for getting off the bus and going inside; all I know is that the drivers' short rest break turned into an hour-long restroom and refreshments stop for our players.

"Nice idea," I said to Tim sarcastically. "This has been great. Thank you."

Tim just smiled and with tongue in cheek said, "I told you it would be a great bonding experience."

I remember someone saying, "Hey, this is great! It feels like I'm back in junior college taking a nineteen-hour bus ride to play in Kansas."

Another player asked me, "Coach, does the number one team in the country really have to bus six hours home from a game?"

Actually, the trip did turn out to be a fun and memorable experience. Of course, it didn't hurt that we had just won the game and were 9–0. But it felt like one of those old-fashioned trips home from a high school game where the coaches and players are together, sharing laughs and a good time.

DEFENDING CAMERON

Despite the win, we dropped from first to second in the BCS rankings, a slight margin behind Oregon. But we still had a solid position in the top two spots, and it would have taken a loss for us to drop below second. Our third and final nonconference opponent—Chattanooga—was next on our schedule for our homecoming game, but before game time arrived, a controversy began brewing.

On Thursday, two days before the game, reports starting surfacing questioning Cameron's recruitment coming out of junior college. We knew we had done nothing wrong during the recruiting process. If we'd had any level of concern regarding Cameron's eligibility, we would not have put him on the field and risked forfeiting games for playing an ineligible player.

With all the talk and speculation regarding that situation, we tried to keep Cameron and our other players focused on football. We did the best we could and defeated Chattanooga 62–24. We led 48–14 at halftime, allowing us to give playing time to a lot of guys in the second half of our homecoming game. Cameron played only the first half but passed for a season-high 317 yards and four touchdowns, and he also ran for a touchdown.

We were 10–0 and down to the final two games of the regular season, against rivals Georgia and Alabama.

The Thursday before the Georgia game, the agent cited in the previous week's reports claimed in a radio interview that he and Cameron's father had met with two Mississippi State assistant coaches. That report set off speculation that Cameron would be ruled ineligible to play against Georgia.

Athletic director Jay Jacobs and I had both defended Cameron earlier in the week, and when this second report came out, we maintained our position: Auburn had done nothing wrong in recruiting Cameron. Cameron was our quarterback, and he would continue to be our quarterback.

Still, accusations were being made—and publicized—that sought to incriminate Auburn.

I understand the media have a job to do, and frankly, if we play poorly or coach poorly, a responsible level of criticism is to be expected. We are in the entertainment industry, after all, and if we don't perform well, we know we will be taken to task. That's part of the business.

My complaint comes when some individuals in the media engage in irresponsible journalism that destroys someone's reputation. It takes a long time to repair a reputation, and sometimes that damage is impossible to recover from. In this case there were a lot of assumptions being made and criticisms being spun out of those assumptions; it was harming Cameron's reputation.

Yet through all the speculation and all the insinuations, Cameron showed an incredible focus that few mature adults—let alone college students—could have maintained. In addition to the recruiting controversy, he was also dealing with the frenzy of media attention that goes with being favored to win the Heisman.

In the midst of everything, football became Cameron's place of refuge. When he was in our offices, in our meeting rooms, and on our practice field (which are all off limits to media), he could get away from all the distractions and just be an Auburn football player. The other guys were very respectful and supportive of him throughout this ordeal. They were good teammates to him, and he was a good teammate to them—as he had always been.

One of the most frustrating parts of the controversy for me was that most of the people who were criticizing Cameron had never met him. I was around him every day, and I knew his character well. At Auburn Cameron had proven himself to be a great Christian kid. In interview after interview, he would take the opportunity to thank God for his abilities and the chance he had been given to play football.

He was a fine role model for his teammates. He didn't drink alcohol. He worked hard. He was smart, and he had a big heart. In one of my first meetings with Cameron, I asked him what he wanted to do if football didn't work out for him. His answer: "I want to open a day care center."

Cameron loved being around kids. He always looked for chances to spend time with my son, Cally, and the other coaches' kids. I think Cameron would just as soon walk past adults and talk with kids instead.

About five or six weeks into the season, I found out that Cameron had been volunteering at an elementary school. He had worked it out with the school, and he spent time every Monday with a small group of kids with behavior problems. None of us knew he was doing that. The media didn't know about it either. That's just how Cameron was—quietly finding ways to use his position as an Auburn football player to make a positive impact.

That's the Cameron Newton I had come to know in our program.

THE COMEBACKS CONTINUE

Cameron's ability to focus in the midst of outside distractions shone through again in the Georgia game.

As we had done many times throughout the season—too many times if you're the head coach—we fell behind early. We scored on our first possession, but Georgia came back with touchdowns on its first three possessions to take a 21–7 lead late in the first quarter. We scored on our first and last drives in the second quarter to tie the score 21–21 going into halftime.

Both offenses moved the ball well in the third quarter, and we started the final period with a 35–31 lead. Cameron led us on two fourth-quarter scoring drives, throwing for the first touchdown and rushing for the second. He would finish the game with 151 rushing yards and two touchdowns on a whopping thirty carries, and he completed twelve of fifteen passes for 148 yards. Onterio McCalebb accounted for our other three touchdowns, all on rushes.

We won 49–31, clinching at least a share of the SEC West Division Championship and securing a spot in the conference championship game three weeks after the Georgia game. But before the championship game was our personal date with Alabama.

As was the case the year before, we didn't have a game the weekend before meeting Alabama on the day after Thanksgiving. Unlike the previous year's Iron Bowl, this time we were the undefeated team with our sights set on a national championship. At 9–2, Alabama was number eleven in the BCS standings. The Crimson Tide—the defending national champions—were out of the running for the national title game, but nothing would have thrilled their fans more than for their team to knock us out of the championship picture.

There's a ton of pressure surrounding the Iron Bowl each year, but with the stakes so high for us, the players felt more pressure than usual during the two-week buildup. With Alabama having won twenty consecutive games at its Bryant-Denny Stadium, we were walking into about as big a challenge as we could face. I tried to defuse the pressure and emphasize a mind-set of "Let's just be who we are."

We came out and got outplayed early. Alabama scored touchdowns on its first three drives, and we didn't gain a single first down in the first quarter. The second quarter started with us trailing 21–0.

What I consider the key play of the game occurred the next time Alabama's offense was on the field. With the ball at Alabama's forty, Mark Ingram, the 2009 Heisman Trophy–winning running back, caught a pass over the middle of the field, broke a tackle, cut to his right, and broke free down our sideline. Inside our thirty-five, Ingram slid left to try to avoid Zac Etheridge. Zac reached out with his right arm and caught a piece of Ingram's right leg. Ingram stumbled for about ten yards; then defensive end Antoine Carter caught Ingram from behind.

As Antoine grabbed Ingram with his left arm, he used his right hand to punch the ball out of Ingram's arm at about the twenty. The ball flew forward and bounced along the sideline and into the back of the end zone, where Demond Washington recovered for a touchback. From where I was standing along that same sideline, I couldn't believe the ball had tightroped the sideline without going out. Nine times out of ten, the ball would have bounced out of bounds somewhere before the goal line and Alabama would have kept possession inside our twenty. I'm convinced that play changed the game because if Alabama had gone up four touchdowns on us at their place, that would have been a steep hill for us to climb.

Late in the first half, we were finally able to put together a good drive that ended with a touchdown pass from Cameron to Emory Blake, and at halftime we trailed 24–7.

During the break I told the players, "This is not an Alabama problem. This is an Auburn problem." I looked at the guys one by one. "So here's what we're gonna do. We're gonna go out and take the ball on the first drive, and we're gonna score. We're going to make it a ten-point game. And then we're going to come back and win it, because with what we've been through in the last eleven weeks, a ten-point game is *nothing* for us. *Nothing.* We know what they're trying to do to us, and it's real simple. We've gotta go out there and outplay them after we make this a ten-point game. This is not complicated."

On our second play after halftime Cameron hit Terrell Zachery for a seventy-yard touchdown pass. Just like that—just as we had discussed at halftime—it was a ten-point game. Now all we had to do was outplay them.

That's what our guys did. We just hammered at them and hammered at them until we took the lead and won.

Cameron scored on a one-yard run to make it 24–21 Alabama with less than five minutes left in the third quarter. The Crimson Tide kicked a field goal on their next possession to give them a 27–21 lead. Our offense came right back with a beautiful drive on our next possession. We chipped our way down the field, not breaking any long plays but steadily marching downfield. With 11:55 left to play, Cameron threw a seven-yard touchdown pass to tight end Philip Lutzenkirchen. Wes Byrum's extra point gave us a 28–27 lead. We had come a long way from being down 24–0.

Now it was up to our defense to win the game.

Alabama's offense answered like you would expect from a defending national champion. They drove down the field to set up a first down at our thirty-four yard line, right on the edge of being in position to attempt a go-ahead field goal. Our defense, though, came up big. Neiko Thorpe and Josh Bynes tackled Ingram for a two-yard loss on first down. The next play was an incomplete pass; then on third down, T'Sharvan Bell sacked quarterback Greg McElroy for a four-yard loss to our forty. Pushed back out of field goal range, Alabama had to punt with 5:18 left.

Our offense kept the ball until only fifty-one seconds remained, when we punted to Alabama's nineteen. Alabama attempted four passes, but all were incomplete. By the time the clock expired, we had set the school record for largest deficit overcome in a victory. In a nod to the never-quit attitude our players had displayed all season, it was our eighth come-from-behind win of the season and the fourth time we had won after trailing by at least ten points.

A WELL-DESERVED HONOR

The conference championship game, to be held a week later at the Georgia Dome in Atlanta, would be a rematch with South Carolina. With a 9–3 record, the Gamecocks were the East Division champions, and they were sitting at number nineteen in the BCS standings. Back in the top spot in the BCS standings after the Alabama win, we just had to win one more game to play for the national title. But first we had to deal with one more round of eligibility issues concerning Cameron.

On Monday the NCAA ruled that a violation of amateurism rules had occurred. Schools are required to declare ineligible any player found out of compliance with NCAA rules, so we followed proper procedures and declared Cameron ineligible. However, we immediately filed an appeal with the NCAA, and Cameron's eligibility was reinstated.

After weeks of speculation, the NCAA made a statement that I was happy to see released. It was especially gratifying to see this part of the release in print: "Based on the information available to the reinstatement staff at this time, we do not have sufficient evidence that Cam Newton or anyone from Auburn was aware of this activity, which led to his reinstatement. From a student-athlete reinstatement perspective, Auburn University met its obligation under NCAA bylaw 14.11.1. Under this threshold, the student-athlete has not participated while ineligible."

Finally this part of the story was behind us.

When we had played South Carolina in late September at Jordan-Hare, we had fallen behind 20–7 in the second quarter before rallying to win 35–27. We were confident about the rematch. We had gone back and studied film of the previous game enough times to see that we could have won by two or three touchdowns if we hadn't made so many mistakes. We reevaluated everything we had done in that game and came up with our best expectations for what South Carolina would try to do against us.

We got off to a good start this time, scoring on our first three possessions to take a 21–7 lead in the first quarter. A fifty-one-yard Hail Mary pass that was deflected but snagged by Darvin Adams on the last play before halftime gave us a 28–14 lead. We scored the first time we had the ball in the third quarter and again about thirty seconds later on an interception return for a 42–14 lead that, for all intents and purposes, put the game away.

It was our best-played game of the season, and perhaps Cameron's too. He accounted for six touchdowns, four passing and two rushing, in a performance that once again had me marveling at his ability to block out the distractions that had been swirling around him for a full month now. In my opinion, he had already locked up the Heisman Trophy.

A week later in New York City, Cameron was officially announced as winner of the Heisman, joining Pat Sullivan (1971) and Bo Jackson (1985) in the tradition of Auburn players to be named best player in college football. Cameron was a runaway winner, receiving 729 of the 886 first-place votes. (By the way, we had a Tiger Walk with several hundred alumni and fans in Times Square before the Heisman ceremony!)

Two nights after the ceremony, at the Heisman Trophy dinner, Cameron displayed the smile and personality that had so impressed me the first time he visited our campus. It was touching to hear him thank his parents and tell those in attendance how his mother and father had raised him to be the best person and the best football player he could be.

Those of us who were in New York City with Cameron for the weekend were proud of how he conducted himself during the different functions. He was truly humbled by the honor and grateful to the people who had helped him along the way. Over the entire weekend of Heisman activities, I think he thanked everyone but himself.

At the dinner I was reminded of when the coaching staff was discussing whether we should recruit Cameron early on. Coach Malzahn and Coach Luper had been two of the people pestering me to reconsider looking at a junior college quarterback. When I finally gave in and told the coaches we could recruit Cameron, I added that if Cameron came to Auburn, he would be Gus's responsibility on and off the field. "His name will be Cameron Malzahn," I had said. "You got me? He's yours."

As we sat there at dinner reminiscing, one of the coaches said to me, "Hey, Coach, you remember what you told us about Cameron?"

I knew exactly where they were going. "Yeah," I shot back. "You talking about the time I told you that when he came to Auburn, his name would be Cameron Chizik?"

When we returned home from New York City, we had about a

month before we would face Oregon in the BCS Championship. I thought I needed to have one more talk with Cameron.

"Okay," I told him, "you have won the Heisman. I won't even get into the conversation yet about whether you're going to stay one more year or go to the NFL. But you've won the Heisman. Your job now is to win the national championship with your team. So let's make sure we're on the same page with what your goal is."

"Coach," he replied, "I'm all in. We're going to win the national championship."

15

THE BEST

Just call on me, brother, when you need a hand
We all need somebody to lean on
I just might have a problem that you'd understand
We all need somebody to lean on

We had been singing those words as a team for four months now. But on this night, the eve of the BCS Championship Game, singing "Lean on Me" had never carried so much meaning.

We had just finished our team meal. Everyone stood, put their arms around each other, and began singing together. Since we'd started this tradition for the Mississippi State game, the song had become *our* song. The words had gradually taken on more significance to the players and coaches because we really had been learning to lean on each other as our undefeated regular season progressed.

Tonight, less than twenty-four hours before we would take the field against the Oregon Ducks, emotions were running high, and it wasn't just about football. The almost two dozen seniors were realizing this was the last time we would sing together before a game. Those seniors had been through difficult times during their stay at Auburn. They had truly leaned on each other throughout their careers.

In addition to the seniors who were leaving, there was a sense that Cameron Newton, our offensive leader, and Nick Fairley, our defensive leader, were playing their last game as Auburn Tigers. They were juniors, but they were projected as first-round NFL draft picks, which meant they would have the option of leaving school for the NFL. Although we didn't know then how their plans would pan out, it was a real possibility that this would be their final game with us.

And then there was the simple fact that we were here in Glendale, Arizona, with a perfect 13–0 record, playing for the national championship. As much as all teams begin preseason practices with the goal of being where we were, when we reflected on all the close games we'd played and all the comebacks we'd made and all the adversity we'd overcome to reach that point, we knew very well that this could be a once-in-a-lifetime opportunity.

As we sang the final lines of the song, I sensed something different in the room that night that I can't quite put into words. *Wow,* I remember thinking. *This is it. This is the last time we're ever going to be together. This is the last time we're going to sing this song as a team.*

I think everyone felt we were sharing a this-is-it moment.

There's no way, I said to myself, *we're gonna lose this game.*

PEAKING AT THE RIGHT TIME

We had thirty-seven days from the SEC Championship Game to the BCS title game. Thirty-seven days. That was eleven more days than the time we have to practice in the spring. And six more days than the time from the beginning of our preseason practice to our first game of the season.

The long gap offered our initial coaching challenge. The way I saw it, we faced two options.

First, we could use the five weeks to get in a lot of work with our younger guys and begin preparing them for next season, in addition to getting ready for Oregon. The players would be between semesters the majority of that period, so we could spend just about as much time on football as we wanted to.

The second option was to look at the time solely as a chance to win the national championship. We wouldn't worry about the potential benefits for the future; instead, we'd focus entirely on the coming game.

We decided on the second option. We were going to prepare with one thing in mind: to win the national title. We were going all in for the championship.

Our biggest challenge would be to build up the team through the thirty-seven days so we peaked for the championship game. We had to find a way to avoid overpracticing or underpracticing the guys.

My first thought was *Man, we can keep them on the practice field for two and a half, three hours every day.*

I knew our football team inside and out. I knew what they responded to and what didn't work. This group of players performed best when being told what we were going to do, how we were going to handle our meetings, and how we would manage our practices. The best thing for them was to lay out our plans and then stick to them. One of our team mottoes has always been "Plan your work; work your plan." And that's what we did.

"We will never practice for more than an hour and a half," I told them. "We'll meet, we'll do a walk-through, we'll break, and then when we come back, you're going to practice for an hour and a half. That time is going to be focused and locked in. The pace will be fast and furious, and we're gonna be moving. Let's get our work done in an hour and a half, and then you're outta here."

We also planned to have a bowling night, a movie night, a team dinner, and any other team activities we could come up with. We weren't going to blister them with football every waking moment. We wanted to keep the players loose and treat our preparation for the title game as much like practice for a regular season game as possible.

One of the big questions from the media leading up to the game was how our defense would fare against Oregon's offense. Oregon had averaged forty-nine points per game with a fast-paced, hurry-up offense that some had compared to a fast-breaking basketball team. Oregon liked to snap the ball quickly after the previous play, trying to break big plays by catching defenders out of position. It seemed like Oregon's offense was all our defensive players heard about.

We coaches had to figure out how we could replicate such a distinct tempo for our defense in practices. We decided to run sets of six, eight, and ten fast-paced plays against the defense— a play every nine or ten seconds. That allowed us to work on calling our defensive plays, getting the players lined up, and then executing the defense without wasting any time. It also allowed us to work on the players' conditioning.

As the game drew near, I pointed out to our players how much attention the commentators and media were paying to Oregon's tempo and speed. "Here's what they're missing, and this is what's never mentioned," I said. "This will be a physical fight. And that's where we're gonna beat 'em. We're gonna play SEC physical, downhill, 'Hit them in the mouth' defense and offense. And that's where we're gonna win it. Once you get into the game, everything you've heard about their tempo and speed is gonna become a myth. We'll take the game over and we'll win it because we're going to make it more physical."

TAKING THE LEAD

Oregon had won the Pac-10 championship, and with the BCS National Championship being played in Arizona, a state that has two universities in that conference, we were solidly in Pac-10 country. As part of the bowl festivities, both teams were treated to an NBA game between the Los Angeles Lakers and the Phoenix Suns. When the Ducks were introduced during a break in the action, the fans went crazy cheering for them. When we were introduced, we got booed.

But when I walked out onto the University of Phoenix Stadium field for pregame warm-ups, I was blown away by all the fans wearing our orange and blue. The stadium seated almost eighty thousand, and I'd say there were twice as many Auburn fans as Oregon fans. Each school had received an allotment of roughly seventeen thousand tickets to sell, and each had sold all its tickets. The demand for tickets was so high that this was called one of the most difficult games to acquire tickets for in sports history.

On the field I asked Tim Jackson, "How did all these Auburn people get tickets?"

Tim pointed to a large section of the stadium filled with Auburn fans. "I guess our fans bought all those tickets from the businesspeople who had them."

I understood there were also thousands of Auburn fans outside the stadium who had been unable to purchase tickets. Even so, with all those who made it inside, it practically felt like a home game for us.

We finished warming up and returned to the locker room. About thirty minutes before kickoff, I walked up to Cameron and Nick Fairley. "I want you to be two of the team captains tonight," I said.

"Coach," Cameron responded, "I don't feel comfortable doing that. I wish you'd find a senior because they deserve it. I don't." In that moment, as Cameron humbly turned down this honor, I was reminded that he's the real deal. No wonder I went to bat for him so many times.

Nick reiterated the same sentiment in respectfully declining my offer to be a captain. That showed me how far Nick had come during his time at Auburn.

With both teams' offenses averaging more than forty points per game, I think most fans were expecting a high-scoring game. But it was the defenses that looked best early.

Oregon had the ball first, and we forced a three and out. After the punt Onterio McCalebb rushed for fifteen yards and a first down on our first play. But we were unable to gain another first down and had to punt.

Oregon got one first down on its next possession before Demond Washington intercepted a tipped pass near midfield. Our defensive players came off the field after that series saying the pace of the game seemed much slower than what they had been accustomed to in practice.

On our second play after the turnover, Cameron threw an interception. Oregon moved the ball to our twenty before Zac Etheridge dove to pick off a pass and stop the scoring threat.

We had to punt a second time after gaining only one first down. When the first quarter ended with the score at 0–0, Oregon had a third and two at our three yard line. Nick made a big play there, tackling the quarterback for a six-yard loss, and Oregon had to settle for a field goal and a 3–0 lead.

Up to that point I thought we looked rusty on offense, possibly because of the long break between games. But we came back with our best drive of the game so far, and Cameron threw a thirty-five-yard touchdown pass to Kodi Burns that gave us a 7–3 lead.

We pinned the Ducks at their seven yard line on the following kickoff, but they connected on an eighty-one-yard pass on the first play. That led to a touchdown pass, and Oregon converted a two-point run to lead 11–7.

After the kickoff, our offense picked up right where it had left off on the previous possession, and we drove all the way to Oregon's nine. A seven-yard pass on first down moved us to the two. Michael Dyer was stopped for no gain on second down; then Cameron was held to a one-yard run on the next play. With fourth and goal at the one, we decided to go for it. We called a pass play that we hadn't run all season but that had been successful every time we ran it the year before. We knew the receiver would be wide open, but Cameron underthrew the pass, and we gave the ball to Oregon at the one.

Then our defense made a big play. After an illegal motion penalty moved the ball a few inches closer to Oregon's goal line, Mike Blanc tackled Oregon's ballcarrier in the end zone for a safety, bringing the score to 11–9. Scoring points on defense can be a momentum changer, and it certainly was in that case.

With good field position following the free kick, we mixed passes by Cameron with runs by Michael to bring us to Oregon's thirty; then Cameron completed a thirty-yard touchdown pass to Emory Blake along the sideline that gave us a 16–11 lead with 1:47 left in the first half.

That score held as we went into halftime.

Our defense had played great, but our offense, though obviously capable of moving the ball, had missed some scoring opportunities. Although we were winning the battle for field position, we weren't winning on the scoreboard by the margin I felt we should have been. To our advantage, though, Oregon's offense wasn't playing at the tempo we had expected. They were having trouble blocking our defensive front seven, and that was preventing them from successfully running the ball as they had in their other games. They seemed to know they couldn't run the ball on us, and looking back, I believe that could have been the game changer.

Most important, we were playing a physical game, just as I'd instructed the guys to do. In the locker room at halftime I revisited the theme we'd talked about in practices. I told the players the second half was going to be old-fashioned football—tough, physical SEC football—and that would be to our advantage. I told them that eventually we would wear Oregon down.

THIRTY MINUTES TO A TITLE

We didn't change anything about our game plan coming out of halftime. We knew what we had to do—now we just needed to capitalize on the opportunities that came our way.

We started the second half with the ball and drove into field goal range, where Wes Byrum kicked a twenty-eight-yarder to put us up 19–11.

The Ducks gained three first downs, including one due to a penalty against us, on their first possession of the second half. But our defense stopped them after they crossed midfield, forcing a punt.

Our offense went three and out and punted. That's when our defense made a goal-line stand. Oregon drove to our three and after three plays had a fourth and goal at our one. Oregon's coaches chose to go for it instead of kicking a field goal, and they called for a fourth consecutive running play. We stopped them at the one.

Our defense was playing great, and preventing Oregon from scoring on four runs that close to our goal line was huge. That was also the last scoring opportunity for either team until the final five minutes of the game.

Still leading 19–11, we started a possession at our twenty-nine. All we had to do, as we had done so many times in the season, was crank out one of those game-ending drives where we eat up the clock, and the championship would be ours. But on our second play, Cameron fumbled on a run and Oregon recovered. Cameron never fumbles, but one of Oregon's defenders made a nice play, coming from behind and punching the ball out of his arm.

Eight plays later Oregon scored on a short shovel pass to make it 19–17 with 2:33 left. Then Oregon scored on a two-point conversion, which tied things up at 19–19.

Demond returned the kickoff to our twenty-five. When our offense jogged out onto the field, I thought, *Been there, done that—here comes more of the same.* We had driven for the winning score late in the game against Clemson, South Carolina, Kentucky, and LSU, and here we were in the same situation. I knew that in a season filled with comebacks, we'd find a way to win this one too.

I even had a quick flashback to the night before, when we sang "Lean on Me" after our team dinner. There was no way Oregon was going to take this game from our guys. I had absolutely no doubt we were going to get it done.

On our first play Cameron threw a fifteen-yard pass to Emory Blake. Michael Dyer followed with a run that turned out to be one of the biggest plays in a game filled with big plays.

Michael ran for five yards and looked like he had been tackled, but he actually came down on top of the Oregon defender and his knees never touched the ground. Michael rolled off the player and back onto his feet, and everyone on the field assumed the play was over. Even Michael hesitated momentarily, but the officials appropriately hadn't blown their whistles. Our sideline shouted, "Run, run, run!" He did, and he gained about thirty more yards before being tackled. The play was reviewed, and the replay official confirmed that the on-field officials had made the correct call.

Michael's run gave us a first down at the Oregon twenty-three, and with Wes as our kicker, we were in field goal range with just under two minutes remaining.

From that point it was simply a matter of improving our field position to give Wes a shorter kick and then letting time run out. Michael ran for four more yards on our next play, and Cameron followed with a two-yard run.

On third and four from the seventeen, Michael carried the ball up the middle and appeared to have broken through a tackle at the one to score a touchdown. But the replay official took a look at the play and ruled him down at the one. That set us up to run down the clock to the final seconds and send Wes out to win the game.

The kick would be from nineteen yards. It was a no-brainer that Wes was going to make it because he is automatic on kicks inside thirty yards. This kick would be a chip shot.

As we were lining up for the field goal, I was standing on our sideline thinking, *He's gonna kick this thing and we're gonna be the national champs.* I thought back to our win in the Outback Bowl the previous season and how that had started our theme of going from good to great. I remembered everything we had been through with Cameron the last half of the season. I thought about all the close games we had found a way to win. I recalled how two years earlier nobody would have guessed that a 5–19 coach would be one play from celebrating a national championship. I promised that after this game I would publicly give credit to God for all that had taken place, just as I'd committed to doing years ago if I ever found myself in this spot.

Everything on the final play was perfect—Josh Harris's snap from center, Neil Caudle's hold, and Wes's kick.

Then all I remember is raising my hands straight up and starting onto the field in what felt like some sort of zombie walk. I was watching our players storm the field, and I felt goose bumps all over my arms. *Did this really just happen?* I kept asking myself.

And then I was trying to find Oregon coach Chip Kelly to congratulate him on a great season and a well-played game.

While all this was taking place, the blood was pumping so hard in my head and ears that I couldn't hear a single thing. It was as though everything inside the stadium were quiet, although I know that wasn't the case. Even today I'm hesitant to try to describe how I felt because any explanation I could give would cheapen the moment.

One thing is for sure: I will never forget what it was like to be the coach of Auburn's national champion team that day. And I certainly wouldn't mind experiencing that again.

REMEMBERING WHAT'S IMPORTANT

As I stood on the stage that had been brought onto the field for the trophy presentation, my thoughts flashed back to how many times I'd watched this moment on television, witnessing the head coach of a team accepting this award. It was almost surreal now that I was the one about to receive the crystal football trophy and hand it to my players.

I thought about how cool it would be if my dad could see this. I knew he'd be proud.

I realized how much of a God moment this was—he was the only reason I could be standing up there as Auburn's coach. There was no other way this whole thing could have happened. I remembered watching the National Championship Game the previous year and saying to myself, *One day I'm gonna be up there. I don't know how long it will take, but one day that's what we're going to be able to do. And it won't be because of me.*

I looked out and captured an image of the Auburn fans celebrating throughout the stadium. They deserved this after waiting fifty-three years since the school's last national championship. I wished I could have seen Toomer's Corner at that moment. I knew toilet paper had to be flying everywhere.

I knew what this victory meant to the Auburn family, and it gave me a great sense of satisfaction to know that so many Auburn fans all across the country were enjoying this and celebrating with us.

When we were all back in the locker room, I gathered the players around. "Listen to me now," I began. "I don't even know what to say about this group. You seniors—you're the reason we're here. What you guys have been able to do just blows my mind. And for you young guys right now, I want you to understand that there's got to be some more of these around the corner. I don't know how we'll do it. We've got to start all over. But we'll figure out a way. But I'm gonna say this: I couldn't be more blessed to be a part of you guys. You know what? You're champions. You're football champions, and I hope you understand how to be a champion father, a champion husband, a champion in whatever you do when you leave here."

I wanted the players to know what it felt like to be great, to be the national champions, to be the best at their trade. But I also wanted them to know it didn't end there. My message to the players was that up to that point, this was the most important event in their athletic careers. But they shouldn't let it be the most important event in their lives.

When I concluded my thoughts, Wes Byrum led us in our postgame ritual of singing the school's "War Eagle" fight song; then we packed in close together, placed our arms around each other's shoulders, and for one last time—but for the first time as national champions—sang "Lean on Me."

CHAMPIONS

One of my favorite aspects of team sports is that within a team victory, there are many individual victories. As I looked around our locker room, I was struck by how many personal victories were represented in our program.

There was Lee Ziemba, who could have gone to the NFL after his junior season and most likely would have been drafted. But he chose to stay at Auburn for his senior year. "Lee," I told him when he informed me he would be returning to Auburn, "I am so proud you're staying. You know, something really big is gonna happen, and this is going to be a great year."

A couple of months after that conversation, he and I were eating lunch, and I asked Lee if he was glad he'd stayed. "Coach," he told me, "it's the best decision I've ever made. I'm as happy as I've ever been in my life." Lee was a great offensive lineman for us, and he was on our line for the final play, blocking two players on the game-winning field goal.

Then there was Wes Byrum, who had made the final kick. After I first arrived, Wes and I had to have a few heart-to-heart talks because I didn't feel he was where he needed to be as an Auburn man. In fact, I temporarily put him on curfew. But Wes was a different young man when he came back from an off-season mission trip to the Dominican Republic. He's an example of someone who had a really good heart but was involved in what I call trivial pursuit. He was pursuing things that really didn't matter in the big picture, but he was able to redirect himself and get his life on course. Wes became someone I trusted not only as a kicker but also as a person.

Neil Caudle was a highly recruited high school quarterback in our state. Neil didn't play much in his four years at Auburn, and he was heading into his senior season when Cameron Newton came in and won the starting job. Neil could have played quarterback at a lot of other schools in the country, but he wanted to stay and finish his career at Auburn. He was a spiritual leader for our team and the kind of guy you would want your son to grow up to be. Neil was our holder on placekicks, and anytime you see a photograph of the ball leaving Wes's foot on the last play of the Oregon game, you'll see Neil, number 19, with his head down and his left hand extended, playing a major role in our championship-winning field goal.

I've told you about Zac Etheridge's miracle. For all intents and purposes, his career should have been finished a year earlier. He shouldn't have been on any field that season, much less in the championship game. But he and his mother said only God would make the decision whether Zac would return to the field, and Zac was out there making a big interception early in the game when Oregon was in scoring position.

At the beginning of the season I wasn't sure if Nick Fairley would be a good teammate. But as the season proceeded, his heart softened and he matured as a man. By the time we took the field against Oregon, Nick had become not only a great player but the kind of person and teammate we hoped he would be. He was now a great personality on our team.

And there was Onterio McCalebb, who had a big touchdown run against Ole Miss and the game-winning touchdown run against LSU. He also had three touchdown runs against Georgia. Onterio's name didn't stand out in the box score for the championship game because his statistics weren't big, but he was a significant part of the reason we were there in the first place. He'd been through a lot in the past few years. His mom had been battling cancer. His family's house had burned down. He had younger brothers and sisters still in school he was concerned about. Onterio had sat at my desk in tears numerous times because he felt like he needed to be at home with his family. He had been told he wouldn't make it in college, but he had a 3.0 GPA while carrying a personal load most would have crumbled under.

Kodi Burns was the ultimate Auburn man. He had lost his chance to become the starting quarterback at the beginning of my first season. Not only that, but we had moved him to a different position. Yet Kodi set an example in his willingness to do whatever the coaches asked for the good of the team. What most people don't realize about Kodi is that he blocked more as a receiver than he ever got the ball. When we ran the ball on the perimeter to his side, we knew he would block his assigned defender. He wasn't just into catching touchdowns; he was also willing to do the dirty work. It was Kodi who scored our first touchdown against Oregon, and that seemed fitting. It was as though you could see the direct results of God's plans for him.

And of course there was Cameron Newton, who had gone through so much—the accusations, the speculation, the negativity. He finally had the chance to fulfill what he'd told me when we made him the starting quarterback: "I want to win it *all*. I want to win the national championship." And here he was, a little over eight months later, having won the Heisman Trophy and the national championship.

At every locker there were stories like these of young men who had shown themselves to be champions long before we took the field for the National Championship Game.

Among those celebrating was a special man: Jay Jacobs, our

athletic director. He won't say it, but our team's championship was an individual victory for him, too. Jay is a model of character and integrity. He stands for all the right things—for the Auburn way, for everything in the Auburn Creed. From being a walk-on football player here to working his way up through our athletic department all those years, he has shown perseverance every step of the way, and I have high regard for what he has accomplished. He took a chance when he decided to hire me despite the backlash he knew would follow. He is a God-fearing man who runs our athletic department the way he believes is best, and he's not afraid to make tough decisions for the good of the program. He's the guy who makes Auburn football go—make no mistake about it!

TO BE THE BEST

"It's a God thing," I said to the team the night we won the national championship, and it was.

I don't mean to overspiritualize things when I say that. We didn't beat Oregon because we outprayed them; we won the game because we outplayed them. It was a football game, not a spiritual competition. We had to practice hard, we had to do all the preparation, and we had to show up against an excellent opponent.

When I say it was a God thing, I'm not really talking about the game. I watched our players grow through the year as a team and as a family, as well as spiritually. God blessed our team, and I would have said it was a God thing even if we had lost to Oregon or if we had finished the season with a 4–8 record. The only difference is that when you're 4–8, you don't have as many people listening to you as when you're the national champion.

My platform has expanded greatly in the short time since we claimed the BCS title, and along with that comes a responsibility to share the message of how significant God is in my life. It falls in line with the promise I made God years ago—that when I started getting to places where I was in the national spotlight and into positions where who knows how many people were hearing what I said on television, I would not be too bashful or ashamed to say the reason I even had such a platform was because God had handed it to me.

That's what he has done, and that's what I am doing.

The word that keeps coming to mind when I consider my platform is *humbled*. I feel like the same guy who was coaching defensive ends at Middle Tennessee State twenty years ago, and I am humbled that God has placed me in a position I really don't deserve to be in.

As I look back over the journey of the past four years, I'm amazed at the struggles Jonna and I went through during the first two years I was a head coach—the experiences we learned from, the hardships we endured on a daily and nightly basis, the times when our competitive spirits were deflated. But we learned to get up again and not let any type of defeat take over in our hearts. We learned to keep driving and to keep believing God's way is the right way, even when we aren't meeting others' definitions of success. God always delivers, and I'm humbled to see how true that has been in my life.

Wins and losses do not define us or validate us. Nor will they. We always tell our players that if they finish playing here at Auburn and can't say they would do it all over again, we have failed as coaches. If they get to the end of their senior seasons and aren't really sad—win or lose—to think this was the last game they'll ever play with their teammates, then we didn't do our job as coaches.

I witnessed three-hundred-pound guys crying in the corner of the locker room, not because they had just won the national championship, but because they would never be together as a team again. I saw a bunch of players get choked up because even though we had accomplished what we set out to do in the beginning, they didn't want it to end.

College football can be a crazy world. I could be Auburn's head coach one more season or twenty more seasons. My preference is for twenty more years, but I know ultimately that is in God's hands. I will remain faithful to God, and I will trust him. In this uncertain, ever-changing business, I couldn't make it through each day without an unchanging God whose plan for my life remains certain. I know true success is measured by obedience to his standards, not by what any commentators say or by the final win-loss record.

God *is* bigger than 5–19.

OVERCOMING YOUR OWN 5–19

If you are in one of those stretches now when your circumstances are telling you that you are failing, may I recommend, as someone who has been there, four steps for you to follow?

1. Look to see whose dictionary you are using. Are you going by the world's definition of success or God's?
2. Make a copy of Psalm 33:9-12 and display it someplace you will see on a daily basis. Remember that God's intentions can never be shaken. Remain obedient to God because he *will* make his plans happen for you.

3. Don't give in to what my friend Mack Brown calls the impostors. Impostors are all around us, trying to convince us of things that aren't the truth. Choose carefully the people you will listen to and who will be in your circle.

4. Borrow a page from the Auburn Tigers' playbook and be "all in."

Be all in for God. At all times. In all circumstances. Be all in for him in great times, in bad times, in mediocre times. That means not letting circumstances change who you are, what you do, and what you believe in.

If you ever have the opportunity to meet a player from Auburn's 2010 national championship football team, ask him what it means to be all in on the football field. He can tell you what it takes to be the best. And he'll probably want to show you the ring he received for being part of the best college football team in the country.

Championship rings are nice, but they are nothing compared to what God promises for those who are all in for him. "God blesses those who patiently endure testing and temptation. Afterward they will receive the crown of life that God has promised to those who love him" (James 1:12).

Whether you're at the top of your game, with a national championship ring on your finger, or at your lowest point, eyeing a dismal 5–19 record, the question remains the same: will you be all in for God?

AFTERWORD

IN DECEMBER 2008, shortly after being named the new head coach of the Auburn University football team, my husband, Gene, stood before members of the media and declared with quiet confidence, "I am the right man for this job!"

I sat nearby, humbled by the seemingly unbelievable sequence of events that had unfolded in one week's time.

As Gene's wife, I knew that those words were not spoken out of arrogance, egotism, or an inflated sense of self-importance. Rather, they were spoken from the depths of a person's soul, where God himself resides—that place where God whispers, *This is it; this is what I purposed for you from the beginning.*

Such is the story of Psalm 33:9-12, which my husband writes about in chapter 4.

You see, when Gene was a second-year head coach with a 5–19 record, the outside world pretty much declared that there was no way Gene would even be considered for the job at Auburn University, let alone be offered the job. It just didn't make any sense—not to the media, the fans, or the analysts . . . not even to us at first. And yet my husband knew that the God we serve is a God who has no equal, a God who does as he pleases, a God who is purposeful, a God who can and does defy all odds.

God utilized the highly publicized and debated numbers of 5–19 to illustrate to a worldwide audience that the circumstances that surround us have no hold on us. They do not define us, and they have no power to destroy us. And most important, we can cling to the promise that we can do everything through Christ, who gives us strength (Philippians 4:13).

Though the outside world might not have viewed it this way, the first *real* championship game was won in Ames, Iowa, because it was there that God redefined the meaning of success for the Chizik family. It was there that God showed us that as long as you are in the center of his will, you have already succeeded. And it was there that he gave us a crystal-clear perspective of what it really means to be *all in*.

Then he brought us to Auburn.

God declared his glory by using a 5–19 head football coach to lead a group of eighteen- to twenty-two-year-olds to a national championship. He did it by providing a miracle of biblical proportions when Zac Etheridge took the field less than ten months after he had been paralyzed from the neck down for several agonizing minutes. He did it by allowing seemingly insurmountable odds to be stacked against our players in one game after another as they learned to embrace the concept of team over self. He did it by using a recycled and redeemed quarterback who became a living testimony to God's grace. He did it by instilling in our players a belief that they could overcome just about anything, including a twenty-four point deficit on the field of our fiercest rival.

And then in January 2011 he showed the very essence of his face on a football field in Glendale, Arizona, when he used a highly recruited high school quarterback who had determined to be obedient at all costs (even if it required personal sacrifice) as the holder for the kick that won the first national championship for Auburn University in fifty-three years.

Now does that mean that God favors the Auburn football team? No. Does it mean that God ultimately even cares who wins a football game? No. And yet it was on that football field in Auburn, Alabama, where he declared to a captive audience week in and week out, "I can do something big. And I will."

That same God has a purpose for you as well.

Although the 5–19 journey was a personal one for the Chizik family, it is a story that ultimately transcends football. At some point in our lives, every one of us will encounter our own version of 5–19. Ours happened to occur on a football field. For others it might be the diagnosis of an incurable illness, the untimely death of a loved one, a bitter divorce, an unexpected job loss, a bankruptcy, or any other situation that has the outside world looking on and declaring, "So sorry," "That's impossible," "That can't happen," or "There's no hope!"

If you take nothing else away from this book, I hope you remember that God is bigger than any 5–19 season you will encounter, and if you are obedient to him and do your best to stay in the center of his will, you too will witness his awesome power in your life.

In Acts 11:21 Luke says, "The Lord's hand was with them, and a great number of people believed and turned to the Lord" (NIV). Our sincere hope in sharing our journey with you is that perhaps by reading it, you will also come to believe. Not in championship games or in Auburn football, but in a God who will and does show up anywhere he chooses and who shows off anytime he wants to—in our case, and quite possibly in yours, despite the best-laid plans of his people.

God bless,
Jonna Chizik

ACKNOWLEDGMENTS

I WOULD LIKE TO THANK . . .

Jay Jacobs, athletic director at Auburn University, and his wife, Angie. Thank you for being a living testimony to the real definition of courage. You represent all that is good in college athletics. Jay, your character and faith make you the rock of the athletic department.

Tim Jackson, executive associate athletic director, and his wife, Michelle. Tim, thank you for tirelessly and selflessly exemplifying true character and integrity and for showing what it means to be an Auburn man. Your contributions to our team go mostly unnoticed by everyone but me. I am truly grateful for you. Thank you, Mimi, for walking alongside Jonna and me and for being the voice of reason when necessary. Your friendship has been a stabilizing force in our lives for the past two and a half years.

The Auburn football coaching staff and their wives. Thank you for the countless hours you put in for the Auburn family. You are making a generational change both on and—more important—off the football field. I am humbled to work alongside coaches who are the best at their trade, and I thank you and your wives for "doing what we do."

Laura Meadors, my executive assistant and our family friend. I could not function adequately without your running my crazy world. Thank you for tolerating my high-maintenance family and for doing all the work you do for us. You are the best.

Jay Gogue, president of Auburn University. Thank you for your leadership and your continued belief that I am still the right man for the job.

Chette Williams, FCA director at Auburn University. Thank you for your spiritual leadership and the guidance you provide for all of us. Thank you for humbly and quietly making a significant, generational change in every person you encounter and for gently guiding all of us to the only destination that really matters—being all in for Jesus.

Rita Chizik, Pat and Vince Sadd, and Marianne Chizik Bouton, my sisters and brother-in-law. Thank you for the continued love and support you've shown me and my family throughout this entire journey. I know it gets difficult for us to find time to spend together, but know that I love each of you deeply.

Rita Chizik, my mother. Thank you for your unconditional love and for providing me with a living example of hard work. I love you with all my heart.

Gene Chizik Sr., my deceased father. To the one man who has made the biggest impact in my life: thank you for leading a life of honor, integrity, courage, and character. You were truly a man's man. You were the man I hope to one day become. I love and miss you.

Julie and Scott Farley, Jonna's sister and brother-in-law. Thank you for being the calm before and during the storms in our lives. Your friendship and wise counsel have helped us better navigate the insanity of our world. Julie, thank you for being the "sweet" sister.

John and Michelle Nicely, Jonna's brother and sister-in-law. Thank you for your loving support over the years and for allowing the Chizik family a place of restoration and healing by opening your home in Florida every time we needed to take a break.

John and Marilyn Nicely, Jonna's parents (and my head high school football coach at Clearwater High School). First, to Coach Nicely, thank you for teaching me the importance of being a leader both on and off the football field. Thank you for "standing in the gap" after my father passed away. To Grammy and Papa Nicely, thank you for loving us and for helping us raise our three children to become the fantastic human beings they have become.

Mike and Sue Wright, pastors of Cathedral of the Cross in Birmingham, Alabama, and Gateway Community Church in Auburn, Alabama. Thank you for your friendship and your spiritual mentorship. Your influence is the reason I am continuously trying to move forward in my walk with the Lord. You guys inspire me, and I look up to both of you as my spiritual leaders.

Mack Brown, head football coach at the University of Texas. Thank you for showing me how to make my way through the crazy world we live in. I appreciate your friendship, your leadership, and the great advice you have given me along this journey. You have advised me on how to provide a functional working atmosphere in a potentially dysfunctional profession.

Bill Reeves, my book agent. Thank you for your willingness to represent Jonna and me in our endeavor to be obedient in sharing the importance of being all in in life. The way you campaigned behind the scenes to share the story of 5–19 is a debt we will never be able to repay.

Carol Traver at Tyndale House Publishers. Thank you for your patience, guidance, and advice along the way. You have been so helpful with navigating us through the uncharted territory of writing a book. Your input has been extremely vital, and the time you invested in this project is very much appreciated.

David Thomas, cowriter of *All In*. Thank you for obediently writing the story *Remember Why You Play*, which allowed God to perfectly prepare you "for such a time as this." Your contribution to our story goes way beyond putting words onto paper. Thank you for articulating our message of faith and for playing the role that God ordained for you from the beginning of time.

Nancy Davis and Kim Hudson, the legal team for YouTurn, LLC. Thank you for all the legal counsel you provided for us as we moved forward with this book. We are also grateful for the role you played in turning our vision of YouTurn into a reality.

The Auburn football family and fans. Thank you for always being all in. I am humbled to be the leader of the Auburn University football team. You are the best fans in the entire country. Thank you for your passionate support and for being one of the biggest reasons we are the 2010 national champions. You are the reason we do what we do and the reason Auburn University is different from anywhere else.

To every unmentioned individual—personal or professional—who has been instrumental in helping me and my family along this journey. You have been responsible for molding and shaping our lives in many ways—some big, some small, but all important and relevant. My family and I acknowledge and appreciate your place in our lives. We are blessed to know you and are forever grateful for what you mean to us.

Now It's Your Turn!

Jer 29:11

All over Alabama thousands of children are currently experiencing their own 5–19 seasons of life. Some are fighting cancer. Some are living in poverty. And others are trying their best to survive in broken or abusive homes.

In 2011 Gene and Jonna Chizik established YouTurn, an LLC devoted to helping nonprofits that positively impact the lives of children throughout the state of Alabama.

If you would like to be "all in" and help support disadvantaged children through YouTurn, please send a check or money order made out to YouTurn, LLC, to:

YouTurn, LLC
Attention: Jonna and Gene Chizik
300 N. Dean Rd. Ste. 5-182
Auburn, AL 36830

Or, for more information, e-mail Jonnachizik.You-Turn@hotmail.com.

CP0484